P9-CQN-992

Educational Sociology:

An Approach to Its Development as
a Practical Field of Study

THE LIBRARY OF EDUCATION

A Project of The Center for Applied Research in Education, Inc.

Categories of Coverage

I	II	III
Curriculum and Teaching	Administration, Organization, and Finance	Psychology for Educators
IV	**V**	**VI**
History, Philosophy, and Social Foundations	Professional Skills	Educational Institutions

Educational Sociology:

An Approach to Its Development as
a Practical Field of Study

GALE EDW. JENSEN

Professor of Education
The University of Michigan

The Center for Applied Research in Education, Inc.
New York

Library of Congress
Catalog Card No.: 65-25730

PRINTED IN THE UNITED STATES OF AMERICA

Foreword

Sociology has many uses although the specifics of each are not always made clear. One area of prolonged controversy has had to do with the relationship of sociology and education. There are two distinct aspects of relationship which are not always recognized: the use of sociology in education and the use of education in sociology. Professor Jensen deals with this controversy in this book.

Sociologists have come to realize that education is a clear-cut and interesting social system within which it is relatively easy to test hypotheses, to observe phenomena of human relationships, and to study social organization. The developments of the sociology of education have made a significant contribution to sociology.

These developments have also been of substantial assistance to educators because the success of the education enterprise depends upon the functions it fulfills in society, the value that members of society place upon these functions, and the confidence they have in the educational institutions which carry out these functions. The current expansion of the education enterprise testifies to the growing recognition of the essential place of the educational functions in society and the consequent necessity for greater investment in the institutions and programs of education in this interdependent relationship.

The day-to-day operations of education with which the educator must cope, however, focus his attention on a different order of things: How can the interest and imagination of those in this particular class of students be captured? Why are there discipline problems in one group, but not in another? What qualities in teachers are most effective in the various particular school situations? Which is the most efficient way of organizing this school system in terms of needs, resources, and community backing? How can this particular institution meet its educational obligations to adults? Which young people in this community should go to college? What should be the educational obligations of the particular community to those who do not go to college as well as to those who do? These and the hundreds of other ever present questions have important sociological implications.

Sociology has accumulated much information which bears upon problems such as these although the specific relationship to and implications for the day-to-day problems may not have been considered or pointed out. The task of the educational sociologist is to reach into the vast material of sociology to obtain the facts which are pertinent to each particular educational problem, to interpret these facts in terms of the problem under consideration, and to find their proper place in a fully-rounded solution to the problem. Since education is an enterprise which deals with people, the solution of all its problems lies in a combination of the facts of content, methods, organization (education), the facts of the learning capacities and propensities of individuals and the learning process (psychology), and the behavior of people in terms of backgrounds, relationships, and organization (sociology). So the educational sociologist must work with a group of experts in other aspects of the problem-solving process.

There is a vast difference between using sociological knowledge in the solution of educational problems and studying education as a sociological phenomenon.

Professor Jensen's basic theory of educational sociology is illustrated in two ways: first, by defining several clusters of related educational problems and indicating the kind of sociological knowledge pertaining to each; second, with an interpretation of selected data from the accumulated knowledge of sociology and social psychology of particular importance to educational practitioners in their encounter with the perennial problems of small groups and also of formal organization. This leads step by step through the process an educator must follow to gain an understanding of the sociological aspects of his problem.

This is not a systematic presentation of material which might be considered a discipline of educational sociology. In fact such a comprehensive presentation is not possible at this stage and perhaps never should be because this theory is concerned with the social dynamics of education which, in the nature of the case, are never the same in terms of time or place. What is far better, however, is an approach and a theory which an educational practitioner can build into his thinking so that he becomes conscious of the sociological aspects of educational problems and phenomena in a way that enables him to build from the resources which are available, the educational sociology which is pertinent and crucial to the problem he faces, the experiment he undertakes, the understanding he seeks, and the results of educational activities he hopes to evaluate. Such a tool of thinking and operating is of far greater value than any neatly packaged compendium of sociological knowledge which hopefully could become useful in education at some time or other. Educational sociology is basically a way of analysing and dealing with educational problems by the application of the sociological kind of knowledge to real situations.

The last chapter sets down guide lines to keep research ventures continuously related to the perennial problems of education. Professor Jensen outlines the types of research which are appropriate and the research designs which are proper to make educational sociology develop in logical patterns of increasing usefulness to educational practitioners. The accumulations of study and experience when kept in orderly patterns and in categories of usefulness make possible an ever enlarging scope of organized knowledge and accessible material in the field of educational sociology.

WILBUR C. HALLENBECK
Teachers College Columbia University
Professor Emeritus of Education

Educational Sociology:

An Approach to Its Development as
a Practical Field of Study

Gale Edw. Jensen

Educational sociology made its first appearance in the curriculum for teacher preparation in the first decade of this century. Henry Suzzalo, one of the early American Herbartians and subsequently President of the University of Washington, offered a course with this title about 1907. Apparently he was in revolt against the largely metaphysical educational philosophy current in his time. In offering this course perhaps he was following the pattern of thought laid down by Auguste Comte who seems to have coined the word "sociology" in his *Cours de Philosophie Positive.* Comte distinguished three levels of explanation historically. Earliest explanations were in terms of a supernatural being. Next in point of time were metaphysical explanations where abstract essences were relied on. Finally both these types of explanations gave way to those based on general or scientific laws. It was in this last category that sociology occurred.

In spite of this favoring genealogy educational sociology has had considerable difficulty in establishing itself as an independent educational discipline. The sort of difficulty educational sociology had to overcome can be seen in the definition of educational sociology offered in even the latest edition of the *Cyclopedia of Educational Research.* The most generic definition of the subject there states that it is "concerned with the social factors in education." But so also are social psychology and educational philosophy and other behavioral sciences. As long as this sort of confusion reigned it was obviously problematical how to mark out the boundaries of educational sociology.

One of the great advantages of the present volume in the Library of Education is the attention the author has given to clearly defining the province of his subject. Indeed, he has even made a sharp distinction between educational sociology and the sociology of education. Perhaps with this theoretical analysis together with the substantive materials included, educational sociology will embark on its most productive period.

JOHN S. BRUBACKER
Content Editor

Contents

CHAPTER I

Distinctions Between Educational Sociology and the Sociology of Education

Introduction

Since it was first recognized that there were some connections between sociology as a field of study, on the one hand, and the educational organizations of a society and "education" as a field of study, on the other, there has been confusion about whether the sociology of education and educational sociology were the same or different kinds of study.

The objectives of this book are to examine this confusion, delineating the similarities and differences between these two kinds of study, and to plot the field of educational sociology in terms of its problems, content, methodology, and future. The major portion of the book will be devoted to the second objective; however, this in no way indicates that the first objective is any less important. Unless it becomes possible to disentangle the sociology of education from educational sociology, the writing produced to accomplish the second objective is likely to lose much of its meaning, especially in terms of its implications for professional and graduate training in the field of education and for the planning and implementation of theory construction and research in the field of educational sociology.

The thesis that will guide this work (one which the author has evolved over a period of years) is as follows: educational sociology is concerned with the development of sociological and sociopsychological types of knowledge that have relevancy for or logical connections to problems of educational practice. The key words for setting up an examination of the similarities and differences between educational sociology and sociology of education are *relevancy for* and *logical connections to*. This thesis asserts that not only is the content of the two fields different in many ways, but the end results of their investigations are different too.

Historical accounts of the development of educational sociology indicate that a great deal of confusion and disagreement about its nature has always been present throughout its sixty-odd years of existence. Studies reported by Moore in 1924 and by Lee in 1927 established that courses in educational sociology had little in common with one another.[1] Brookover has developed a set of categories which portray the degree of divergency among ideas about what educational sociology is or should be.[2]

The first of these categories identifies educational sociology "as the means of social progress." This notion seemingly was provided by Lester F. Ward, who perceived education as an "ameliorative agency" with the avowed purpose of improving society.[3] Ward's idea of education as the social mechanism through which social progress was achieved was carried out in the writings of Kinneman, Ellwood, and Good.[4] Brookover states that these writers expounded the thesis that the school could educate people to "exercise social control" so intelligently and skillfully that the level of the culture would be developed to its highest level.[5]

The second category of ideas about the nature of educational sociology was expressed in the writings of Snedden, Finney, Peters, Clements, and Kinneman.[6] This idea was that educational sociology could be utilized to determine the aims or objectives of education. This concept of educational sociology provided a way to formulate a social philosophy of education which utilized educational sociology to make or provide an analysis of society and human needs.

---

[1] D. H. Culp, *Educational Sociology* (New York: Longmans, Green & Co., Inc., 1932), pp. 554–55; Wilbur B. Brookover, "Sociology of Education: A Definition," *American Sociological Review,* XIV (1949), 407–15.

[2] Wilbur B. Brookover, *A Sociology of Education* (New York: American Book Company, 1955), pp. 23–27.

[3] L. F. Ward, "Education as the Proximate Means of Progress" in *Dynamic Sociology* (New York: Appleton-Century-Crofts, Inc., 1924), II, xiv.

[4] Alvin Good, "Sociology and Education," *Harper's,* XXVI (1926), 25; C. A. Ellwood, "What is Educational Sociology?" *Journal of Educational Sociology,* I (1927), 25–30. John A. Kinneman, *Society and Education* (New York: the Macmillan Company, 1932), p. 49.

[5] Brookover, *A Sociology of Education, op. cit.,* p. 24.

[6] Ross L. Finney, "Divergent Views of Educational Sociology," *Journal of Educational Sociology,* I (1927), 100; David Snedden, *Sociology for Teachers* (New York: Appleton-Century-Crofts, Inc., 1924), p. 33; C. Peters, *Foundations of Sociology* (New York: the Macmillan Company, 1935); S. C. Clement, "Educational Sociology in Normal Schools and Teachers Colleges," *Journal of Educational Sociology,* I (1927), 33; Kinneman, *op. cit.,* p. 48.

The third category of ideas conceived of educational sociology as a form of applied sociology. One phase of this approach had to do with the application of sociology to curriculum development. Others, however, such as Francis Brown, did not limit educational sociology as a form of applied sociology to the development of curriculums. In his text on educational sociology, Brown states: "The educational sociologist utilizes all that has been learned in both fields, but joins them in a new science by applying sociological principles to the whole process of education."[7]

A fourth category for conceptualizing educational sociology centered about the analysis of the socialization process. This idea of educational sociology makes the development of personality its central concern. Educational sociology is (1) a study of how the person becomes socialized, and (2) a study of how to manage the educational process so as to insure good personality development. Two writers who have expounded this view are Robbins and Brown.[8]

A fifth category for identifying the nature of educational sociology designates it as a discipline concerned with analyzing the place of education in the community and the society. This approach to educational sociology makes it a study concerned with (1) analyzing the existing arrangements and structures of the community and society, and (2) determining what the function of education should be under these conditions. This idea of educational sociology is manifested in the writings of such persons as Cook, Warner, and Hollingshead.[9]

A sixth notion about the nature of educational sociology conceives of educational sociology as the study of social interactions, both within the school and between the community and the school. According to this approach, educational sociology is concerned with the analysis of patterns of social interaction and social roles within the school organization and with the identification of relationships between students and the groups to which they belong outside the

---

[7] Frances Brown, *Educational Sociology* (Englewood Cliffs, N.J.: Prentice-Hall, Inc., 1947), pp. 35–36.

[8] Florence G. Robbins, *Educational Sociology* (New York: Holt, Rinehart & Winston, Inc., 1953); Brown, *op. cit.*

[9] Lloyd Allen Cook, *Community Backgrounds of Education* (New York: McGraw-Hill Book Company, 1938); A. B. Hollingshead, *Elmtown's Youth* (New York: John Wiley & Sons, Inc., 1949), W. L. Warner, *et al., Who Shall be Educated?* (New York: Harper & Row, Publishers, 1944).

school. Persons who have based their writings on this concept of educational sociology are Waller, Greenhoe, Smucker, Znaniecki, and Wilson.[10]

Bases of Distinction Between Educational Sociology and Sociology of Education

The central purposes of each discipline. Two main objectives guide investigations in educational sociology. First, educational sociology has the task of developing knowledge which has relevancy for problems of educational practice. Many of the problems confronting the educational practitioner are sociological or socio-psychological in character. Systematically formulated sociological knowledge about these problems, however, is extremely scarce and needs to be greatly extended if educational practice is to improve.

Second, educational sociology has the task of formulating knowledge about the sociological phenomena inherently associated with problems of educational practice in such a way that asserted cause-and-effect relationships between educational variables can be identified. Educational practice is based upon *presumed* causes and effects between the actions undertaken by the practitioner and the results desired by the clients he serves. Improvement of practice is contingent upon continual conceptual reformulation, testing, and verification of the presumed cause-and-effect relationships operating between the variables which the practitioner attempts to manage or control so as to attain or achieve a set of specified educational objectives.

On the other hand, the sociology of education is primarily concerned with investigating the sociological aspects of educational phenomena and institutions. The phenomena about which knowledge is to be formulated may or may not prove to be relevant to problems of educational practice. In this case, educational practice does not prescribe the kinds of knowledge that are to be developed. If by chance the result does prove to be helpful to educational practice,

[10] Willard Waller, *Sociology of Teaching* (New York: John Wiley & Sons, Inc., 1932); Florence Greenhoe, *Community Contacts & Participation of Teachers* (Washington, D.C.: American Council on Public Affairs, 1941); O. C. Smucker, "The Campus Clique as an Agency of Socialization," *Journal of Educational Sociology,* XXI (1947), 163–69; Florian Znaniecki, *Social Roles of the Man of Knowledge* (New York: Columbia University Press, 1940); Logan Wilson, *Academic Man* (London: Oxford University Press, 1942).

this is all to the good. The needs of educational practice, however, are only incidental to the purposes of such sociological investigations. The problem being examined is essentially a problem of sociology, not a problem of educational practice.

Furthermore, the form in which the findings of sociology of education studies are summarized is determined, not by the needs of educational practitioners for improving upon the cause-and-effect frameworks they employ to direct their actions but, rather, by the needs of the particular area of sociological study involved. In brief, the form in which knowledge developed from sociology of education studies is stated is not likely to be one which the educational practitioner can use to plan and direct his action. It may, of course, be informative and throw some light on areas of educational endeavor he had not perceived before, but generally it will be of little immediate use in terms of providing improved conceptual frameworks for analyzing problems and planning and conducting action.

Types of problems each discipline entertains. The basic distinction between educational sociology and the sociology of education in terms of the problems they select to investigate is that the problems of the former are obtained from the field of education while those of the latter are obtained from the field of sociology. An examination of the chapter on the sociology of education in the recent publication, *Sociology Today,* makes this very clear.[11] In this chapter, Gross points out that sociologists are beginning to discover that institutions of lower and higher learning provide a fertile field for sociological research and can provide unique laboratories in which to investigate strategic sociological problems.[12] Specifically, Gross asserts that educational systems provide excellent facilities for studying such sociological matters as the socialization process, social mobility, aspiration levels, social and cultural change, structure and dynamics of small social systems, status relationships, role conflict, and adjustment of social systems to their external environment. This same perspective of the relationship of sociology to education is held by Brim.[13]

---

[11] Cf. Neal Gross, "The Sociology of Education," in Robert K. Merton, Leonard Broom, and Leonard S. Cottrell (eds.), *Sociology Today* (New York: Basic Books, Inc., 1959).

[12] *Ibid.,* pp. 129–31.

[13] Orville G. Brim, *Sociology and the Field of Education* (New York: Russell Sage Foundation, 1958), pp. 76–78.

Educational sociology draws its problems from the world of the educational practitioner. The practitioner is confronted with three general kinds of problems. The first of these pertains to the organization of a learning situation for the accomplishment of certain educational objectives. In brief, he is expected to utilize his knowledge as an expert to bring about desired behavioral changes in people. This means that he must understand how the sociological variables which operate in these learning situations affect the educational objectives he is to achieve. It is from situations of this kind that educational sociology draws its problems.

The second of these general types of problems has to do with what the learning objectives "should be." In many senses, the educator is an agent of the total society and is expected to do what is right and needed by that society. As there are always numerous ideological bases and value positions which can be utilized to determine what the proper educational objectives and policies should be, the practitioner is confronted with evolving a normative or direction-setting framework which enables him to make "good" judgments about what sort of educational objectives and policies are the "proper" ones. It is, of course, easy to see that these are extremely difficult and trying problems, not subject to easy solution. One aspect of evolving these normative or direction-setting frameworks, sometimes referred to as *educational policy-making,* has to do with defining and obtaining data about the "questions of sociological fact" which are inherent in the task of developing solutions to this kind of problem. The sociology of education has not had, nor is likely to have, any concern for these types of problems.[14] It is from the "questions of sociological fact" confronting the educational practitioner that educational sociology draws additional problems for study.

The third general type of problem the educational practitioner encounters concerns the selection of the most effective and efficient educational technology available for implementing the educational action prescribed as necessary for accomplishing the educational objectives. Much of the educational technology employed assumes that one particular way for managing sociological phenomena so as to achieve prescribed educational objectives is better than another.

[14] D. A. Hansen, "The Responsibility of the Sociologist to Education," *Harvard Educational Review,* XXXIII (Summer 1963), 312–25.

Very often the educational practitioner wonders whether the assumptions about managing sociological phenomena are correct. In brief, whenever the assumptions about the technological management of sociological phenomena present in educational situations are questioned, new problems for the educational sociologist have arisen. This constitutes another source from which problems for educational sociology are derived.

In summary, it is these three general types of problems faced by the educational practitioner that generates problems to be explored by educational sociology. They impose upon research and theoretical workers in the field of educational sociology the selection and formulation of problems which have logical connections to prescriptive, normative, and technological knowledge needed by the educational practitioner which is essentially sociological in character. These kinds of problems investigate sociological and sociopsychological processes as *instrumental processes* for accomplishing specified educational objectives. In this sense, they are a different kind of problem from that which is investigated by the sociology of education.

The way each discipline orders its units of study. Attempts by any discipline or field of study systematically to investigate the problems in which it is interested require that units of study be established. All the factors or components which comprise the field and which are relevant to a particular problem cannot be studied at any one time. This means that the investigator must place the problem in a setting which eliminates some of the factors or components of the total system. Specifically, this means that the investigator places the problem in a subsystem of the total field. Lazarsfeld speaks of this as the "location of topics." [15] Mostly, this is done unconsciously by investigators and accounts very often for different sets of findings for identical or similar problems.

The point to be made in this section is that for similar or identical types of problems, educational sociology and the sociology of education as disciplines will ultilize different types of units of study. Stated otherwise, similar problems will be studied in different settings. This means that similar or identical problems are not being studied under equivalent conditions. For educational sociology, the components of the unit of study will be comprised of whatever socio-

[15] Paul Lazarsfeld, "Problems in Methodology," *Sociology Today,* III (1959), p. 40.

logical factors the investigator believes are intimately involved in the practitioner's problem. For example, both educational sociology and sociology of education studies are likely to be concerned with questions of fact or "how sociological variables work or operate." The unit of study for the educational sociologists who deal with this type of problem will be organized in terms of discovering "how sociological variables work" in terms of achieving the kinds of educational outcomes with which the educational practitioner is concerned. The sociology of education study, on the other hand, would devise a unit of study which would be concerned mainly with testing a set of theoretical concepts which had been proposed for conceptualizing "how sociological variables work or operate." The unit of study in this instance will be composed of whatever would be required to test a set of concepts.

Types of end-propositions for which each discipline strives. Every discipline has some kind of goal with respect to the kind of end-product it wishes to develop. The goal for educational sociology is different from that of the sociology of education. The end-product of the educational sociologist needs to be utilitarian in character in the sense that it must be something which is usable by the educational practitioner. The educational sociologist is the connecting link between sociologists of all kinds (not only sociologists of education) and the educational practitioner. He has to be familiar with the fields of each and to engage in a "translation" process which enables him to convert one kind of knowledge into another. Stated differently, his client is the educational practitioner and his main supplier of "raw conceptual material" is the sociologist.[16]

More specifically, the end-propositions of the educational sociologist must specify the cause-and-effect relationships between significant sociological variables and certain operational indices the practitioner employs to determine whether satisfactory progress is being made or whether "things are going well." These kinds of end-results might be termed prescriptive cause-and-effect propositions. It is these kinds of cause-and-effect relationships that the practitioner must have if he is to prescribe the kinds of actions that need to be taken to accomplish educational objectives desired by the society and individual clients. Without these, he can rely only on his

[16] Chapter III provides an account of the knowledge-formation process in educational sociology.

past experience and intuitions. It is only when these kinds of cause-and-effect relationships become available to the practitioner that it becomes possible for his profession to advance. It is the goal of the educational sociologist to supply the practitioner with these kinds of propositions—that is, with propositions which pertain to the way sociological and sociopsychological variables affect the development of human behaviors specified by educational objectives.

Furthermore, educational sociology has as its goal that of assisting in the formulation of normative propositions that can serve as bases for making judgments about whether certain educational objectives, policies, and practices "should be" accepted or employed in educational programs. Without the contributions of the educational sociologist, the educational practitioner is unable to develop adequately those aspects of his normative principles for action that have to do with questions of sociological fact. Neither the prescriptive cause and effect nor the normative propositions are considered to be the kinds of propositions that the sociology of education would have as its goal. Rather, it would seek to develop a formal theoretical system about those kinds of sociological problems that could be efficiently studied in educational systems.

One additional difference between the end-propositions of educational sociology and those of the sociology of education pertains to the fact that educational sociology studies technological questions of educational practice. That is, it is concerned with questions about the most effective and efficient ways to manage sociological and sociopsychological variables so that they can act as determinants of educational objectives. These are the kinds of propositions that the sociology of education will not develop at all.

The types of concepts each discipline utilizes. The system of concepts employed in educational sociology is formulated for the specific purpose of dealing with problems of educational practice. There is, of course, a strong likelihood that these concepts will have definitions and interrelationships similar to those used by sociologists who utilize educational systems to explore sociological problems. There is no doubt that the kinds of sociological phenomena involved are likely to overlap. The significant point to be made, however, is that the definitions attached to concepts and the ways in which they are ordered in the work of the educational sociologist are determined by the nature of the problems found in educational practice. In an indirect way, the educational sociologist is interested in building and testing a theoretical system; however, his immediate concern is with finding effective and efficient ways of coping with the problems of practice that constantly threaten to overcome the educational practitioner. In concept-building he is more pragmatic than the sociologist of education. He thinks of a system of concepts primarily in terms of usefulness for dealing with practical problems, and secondarily in terms of "formal niceness" or logical-empirical validity.

A system of concepts utilized by the educational sociologist is always being assessed by three criteria. First, it is judged in terms of its analytic powers—that is, its ability to provide explanations or an understanding of the "practice situation." Second, its worth is determined by its ability to provide a conceptual basis upon which to make decisions as to what should be done and how variables will have to be organized to get it done. Third, it is judged in terms of its power to guide practitioner action toward more effective job performance. These are the criteria that guide the development of concept systems in educational sociology. They place definite limitations on the degree of abstractness that is acceptable for the concepts of educational sociology. The general rule to be followed is: Conceptualization should be abstract only to the point that logical connections can be made between the concepts and the intellectual tasks that lie at the heart of educational practice; viz., analysis, decision-making, and directing action.

The Rationale of the Book

Although a treatise to establish the bases for distinguishing educational sociology from the sociology of education might constitute a partial justification for the time and resources to be allocated to this book, it is certainly not enough, nor is it the most important basis for justification. Much more important is the need to become clear about the nature of educational sociology as a practical discipline so that an effective working structure can be built between educational sociologists and other kinds of sociologists. In sociological terms, we need a job or role analysis and definition that can serve as a perceptual basis for building a structure which differentiates clearly between certain "professional sociological roles" in a way that eliminates the confusion, stumbling, collisions, and competition that now characterize the behavior of educational sociologists with other sociologists, and particularly their cousins from the field of the sociology of education. This is a minimum requirement for organizing an effective knowledge-development system and maintaining a balance between the theoretical and practical aspects of sociological investigation about which Merton speaks in *Sociology Today*.[17]

Assuming that we can free ourselves of the "prestige prejudices" our own socialization has produced, we need to analyze the problems of the production of "educational-sociological" knowledge to determine the kinds of social and formal organization that needs to be created between educational sociologists and other kinds of sociologists so as (1) to facilitate a free flow of information from one area of investigation to another and (2) to instigate effective forms of problem-solving, interractions between various kinds of specialized "knowledge-production" roles.

If such an analysis of role functions and relations could be defined, and if some kind of organizational structure could be developed which orders these roles to one another in keeping with the specified role functions and relations, it is believed that a *quid pro quo* relationship in terms of benefits would be possible. At first, a "real" sociologist might think that the benefits were pretty one-sided and that he is being asked to take on the task of aiding an "underdeveloped" relative. However, those of us who classify ourselves as educational sociologists sometimes are amused at the naïveté and ignorance of a respectable sociologist when he attempts to implement research designs and collect data inside of educational systems. This is sometimes done with such crudeness that the educational sociologist seriously doubts that the investigating sociologists ever obtained the kind of data required by his research problem. The educational sociologist is further amused by the adroit manner in which the data are analyzed and then reported at a later time in a prized professional magazine. Clearly, there is much with which an educational sociologist can aid other sociologists who wish to use educational systems for investigating sociological problems. Were the right kind of working structure established between educational sociologists and other sociologists, these other sociologists would

---

[17] Merton, *op. cit.*, xiv, xxvi.

find the educational sociologists helpful not only when they go to the field to obtain data from the "natives," but also for problem formulation, research design, sampling, data-collection techniques, and instrument-development questions are being entertained. In brief, then, if we wish to build a knowledge-development organization which eliminates the confusion between educational sociology and the sociology of education and creates an effective working structure between educational sociologists and other sociologists, we must establish a clear notion as to the nature of educational sociology as a field of study. If this task can be carried out successfully, it then becomes possible to perceive clearly the nature of the work of the educational sociologist. And if the work of the educational sociologist can be accurately perceived and fully understood, it becomes possible to consider the formation of a knowledge-development organization that should prove to be beneficial to both the fields of sociology and education as behavioral sciences.

This type of analysis also should enable us to surmount a very old conceptual impasse centered around the notion that sociology is a theoretical or basic discipline while education is an applied field or intuitive art. This study should make it very clear that this is an inadequate way to distinguish between the two disciplines. It will become clear that education is no less theoretical than sociology. It should become clear, also, that education is just as basic a discipline as sociology and that similar methods of knowledge-development characterize both fields as behavioral sciences.

Organization of the Book

Because the immediate task is that of analyzing the field of educational sociology for purposes of determining the nature of its content and methodology as a practical discipline, this book will proceed to examine and treat the major phases of such an analysis.

Chapter II will constitute the starting point of the analysis and will be devoted to an examination and description of certain problems of educational practice that have long plagued educational practitioners. These problems will be designated as perennial problems of the educational practitioner that have some relevancy for educational sociology. The problems, as we shall see, are far more numerous than has been supposed. Two general categories will be identified. One of these has to do with the kinds of problems that are generated internally—that is, by the inner organizational structures, interactions, and cultures, of educational systems. The other deals with problems that are provoked by the external environments or community settings of educational systems. The first of these general categories will include problems such as:

1. What are the most effective forms of educational organization?
2. What kinds of styles of administrative behavior are most appropriate for educational systems?
3. How should teachers cope with instructional problems caused by heterogeneous socioeconomic groupings of students and teachers?
4. What are the most effective types of communication relationships to establish between school roles and working groups?
5. How should the distribution of rewards to students and teachers be determined?
6. What conditions produce high turnover and discharges of teachers?
7. What conditions produce high motivation in students to learn and participate in school life?
8. What is the effect of the socialization process upon formal instruction?
9. How do sex relationships between students, teachers, and administrators affect instruction?
10. What should be the norms of proper school behavior for teachers, students, and administrators?

The second category will include such problems as:

1. What should be the relationships between professionals and lay boards of education with respect to the determination of educational objectives, programs, and operating policies?
2. What is the impact of economic and technological change upon educational systems?
3. What is the nature of the economic and sociopsychological relationships involved when an educational system attempts to obtain resources from the community?
4. How does the educational profession develop and establish itself as a recognized profession?
5. What is the affect of political organizations and activity upon educational systems?
6. What provokes attacks by community groups upon educational systems?
7. How do the cultural characteristics of communities determine what kinds of instructional procedures will be effective?
8. How do demographic and ecological change affect educational systems?

9. What is the effect of community social-class structure upon school structure and operation?

The second part of Chapter II will be concerned with identifying the general types of sociological and sociopsychological phenomena involved in these perennial problems. An effort will be made to coordinate the different types of perennial problems with the different types of sociopsychological phenomena. It is by this procedure that the content of educational sociology can be determined. Five general types of phenomena will be identified and discussed.

The first type to be identified will be the small, or face-to-face, group. The most prominent characteristic of present-day forms of school organization has to do with the utilization of the face-to-face group to carry out its programs. The working machinery of the school consists of numerous interrelated groups assigned specific tasks. The collective accomplishments of these different groups are supposed to make possible the realization of the educational objectives set for school systems by their communities. Some of these groups are called *classroom* or *instructional groups;* others are called *teams, orchestras,* or *choirs*. Some are designated *clubs,* and designed to foster special interests involving such things as science, drama, foreign languages, and so on. Some are called *peer groups* and *cliques*. Some are labeled *counseling* and *student-government groups, committees, departments, divisions,* or *offices*. Wherever one goes in an educational system, one finds these various kinds of face-to-face groups. Students, faculty, administrative, maintenance, and service personnel belong to one or more of these groups. It is through these groups that the formal instructional and socialization processes are carried on. Many of the perennial problems to be examined in Chapter II involve group processes. They constitute one of the five basic kinds of phenomena which are in some way involved in all problems of educational practice.

The second type of phenomena to be discussed can be referred to as formal organizations. All educational systems are formal organizations. As a consequence, all educational systems are confronted with the kinds of problems to be found in formal organizations. These are, for example, the typical problems of determining what kinds of specialized roles to create and what sorts of working and communication relationships to establish between them. There are problems of competition between roles and groups of roles for the resources and rewards available within the organization. There are the problems connected with authority and power struggles between different roles. There are problems pertaining to establishing arrangements for different kinds or personnel in decision-making. There are problems of establishing rules, policy, and standards of behavior to which members of the organization should adhere.

The third kind of phenomena that will be identified and discussed will pertain to the socialization process and the way it affects personality formation and change. To some, the social learning that takes place in educational systems is more significant for the community and society as a whole than is formal instruction. It is the learning that emerges from the socialization experiences of a school system that cannot be forgotten and that sets the limitations and potentials of the group. The socialization process thus becomes central to many of the perennial problems of educational practitioners.

The fourth type of phenomena to be discussed in Chapter II can be designated as human communities. It is the community that creates, supports, and shapes an educational system. It does this for the purpose of accomplishing certain life aims to which its members aspire. To the extent that the community has difficulties with its own structure and operation, it can be expected that the educational system it supports will also experience problems that reflect these difficulties. In other words, communities and school systems are interdependent social systems which reciprocally determine one another's welfare. It is for this reason that school-community relations problems become prominent in terms of the extent to which they persist from year to year.

The fifth kind of phenomena to be discussed has to do with the basic social ideas and institutions that underlie, order, and operationally control societies. Examples of some of these social ideas are property, contract, constitutional government, law, and the market. Examples of social institutions are courts, legislatures, and commodities markets. These provide the basic structure of a society. Differences between people about these things provide the materials for the great political, economic, and military struggles that have characterized relationships between societies. They have also provided the ideological material for revolutions and interorganizational struggles within societies. It is with this kind of phenomena that the normative problems become involved because educational objectives and policies must ultimately be examined in light of the basic social ideas and institutions to which a people are committed. Whenever a society is in ferment, is experiencing a high degree of technological and social environmental change, and is discovering that many of its cherished social ideas and institutions do not seem to work very well, the educational system it supports is confronted with a serious dilemma: Is it to continue teaching the old ways, thereby contributing to the society's inability to solve its problems, or is it to explore a new set of ways which the present members of the society may find psychologically upsetting, bizarre, and perhaps unacceptable?

Chapter III will be concerned with describing and analyzing the all-important knowledge-development process in educational sociology. Three distinct procedures are employed. One has to do with the way educational sociology utilizes the knowledge developed by other fields of sociology. This usually requires some kind of reformulation of the knowledge. Sometimes this reformulation is characterized by a systematic and conscious recasting of the ideas and propositions so as to make them more suitable for dealing with problems of educational practice. Most often, however, this is done in an intuitive, nonsystematic way, which employs trial-and-error, "flash-of-insight" procedures to make connections between sociological knowledge and problems of educational practice.

The second procedure can be identified as the formulation of principles which are generalizations based on numerous actual incidents or cases. Certain kinds of problems of educational practice reappear frequently. As a result of dealing with the same problems on numerous occasions and under various conditions, the practitioner notes the presence of certain common elements and the regularities of relationships between these elements. Gradually he comes to expect the presence of these elements and their observed relationships whenever a particular kind of problem appears. As his expectations more and more come to be fulfilled with each appearance of the problem, he becomes more and more certain as to what will happen and what lines of action will produce what kinds of educational results. With this experience he begins to create a conceptual framework which will be coordinated with the actual situation. As he uses this conceptual invention and finds that it serves him well by shortening the amount of time and energy he must give to each situation and by enabling him to act with more certainty as to educational outcomes, he learns or internalizes this conceptual invention so that it becomes a part of his personality. As he becomes ever more certain about the "goodness" of this conceptual invention, he begins to record it; as it becomes available for public examination, the educational sociologist sifts through it and picks out that part which can be incorporated in educational sociology. A good deal of the content which appears in the textbooks on educational sociology has been formulated in this way.

The other procedure that will be outlined is indeed very rare in educational sociology. It is discussed and described because of its great potential for educational sociology rather than to provide an account of how it now functions in connection with the formation of educational knowledge. This particular procedure will be designated the axiomatic method. Because of the great need in educational practice for an understanding of how the significant variables which determine educational outcomes vary and affect one another, this particular method has high potential for the improvement of educational knowledge. It is true that it is more exacting than the methods we now use, but we can learn to understand its fundamental nature and to employ it effectively. Its incorporation in the knowledge-development process of educational sociology could go a long way toward lifting the educational practitioner above the layman with respect to those problems and controversies that involve questions of fact or cause-and-effect relationships. With respect to these kinds of questions, the educational practitioner seems to be no more knowledgeable or certain than the layman. Because of the high potential of the axiomatic method for the knowledge-development process in educational sociology, Chapter III will endeavor to provide an example of its usage. If this particular method of knowledge development could be linked with the borrowing-from-other-sociological-disciplines method and with the generalization-from-practice method, educational sociology could develop in a way that would revolutionize the field of educational practice. Its failure to do this in the past has committed American education to stagnant and inadequate resolutions of problems in such areas as educational organization, curriculum development, instructional procedures, and administration.

Chapter IV will be devoted to outlining the research needs of educational sociology as a developing discipline. These needs fall into two basic categories. The first of these has to do with identifying different types of research problems and the kind of knowledge each produces. The second of these categories is concerned with identifying research strategies and designs that would study these problems in a way that would lead to the formation of the kinds of knowledge needed for effective and efficient educational practice.

Almost no thought has been given to the kinds of research strategies and designs that would be appropriate for building educational sociology. As behavioral science researchers become more sophisticated about the methodological problems of research, it is becoming apparent that the way one goes about investigating a problem determines the kind of findings one can hope to reach. Although the problem and the way it is conceptualized certainly have a strong determining influence upon the end-results of a research project, the operational characteristics of the research design itself determines the kind of end-results that will actually be produced. By this is not meant only that the design must eliminate as much error as possible but, rather, that the design is the operationalization of a problem. The implication of this statement is that the problem actually being investigated is that which is operationalized in the design, and not that which is formally outlined and defined in the research report. The coordination of these two aspects of research in educational sociology has not been given the attention it deserves. Too often a researcher formally outlines and defines a problem and then operationalizes quite a different one in the design of the research. He, of course, obtains findings for the latter—which may be a problem quite different from the one which he believed to be so important and which he really wanted to investigate. Furthermore, the general type of research strategy and approach that is utilized is seldom considered in terms of its effect upon the kinds of interpretations and generalizations that can be formulated from its findings. For example, it is not unusual for a researcher to want to determine whether one significant educational variable has an effect upon others, and if it has, what the nature of these relationships is. He then proceeds to select a research approach (such as an exploratory field-study type of research strategy) which has little probability of even being able to demonstrate clearly whether there are any relationships between the variables being investigated.

Perhaps there are times when there is no choice in the matter of selecting research designs and strategies. At such times, the researcher has to use whatever type of research approach he can make work. At other times, however, he does have a variety of research approaches for studying and handling his variables and then chooses the one which is relatively ineffective from the standpoint of studying the variables of the research in a way required by the problem. When this happens, it becomes impossible to use the findings of the research to formulate the kind of propositions needed to control and manage these variables in practice.

Summary

This chapter has been concerned primarily with identifying and elaborating the ideas and beliefs that will be employed to specify how the field of educational sociology should be developed to enable it to contribute effectively to the work of the educational practitioner. The brief historical review establishes clearly that confusion and disagreement about the nature of educational sociology has been characteristic of its development. To confound the matter further, there has been the difficulty of distinguishing educational sociology from the sociology of education. Between the confusion and disagreement about the nature of educational sociology and the inability to differentiate it from the sociology of education, its development as a practical field of study seems to have ground to an agonizing halt at a time when progress is needed most. The purpose of this book is to cut away some of the intellectual dilemmas and blinders that have immobilized educational sociology and to outline a new and more productive path upon which it might be set. Until this can be done, there is little likelihood that new knowledge of this kind will be developed or that teachers and researchers, who could advance it as a distinct discipline, will be trained.

The major thesis of the book is that educational sociology is concerned with the development of those sociological and sociopsychological types of knowledge that have a logical relevancy for the problems of educational practice. Because the originating points of its studies should be problems of educational practice, educational sociology becomes a field of study that is distinctly different from the sociology of education. To support these assertions, a comparative analysis of educational sociology and the sociology of education were provided in terms of the central purposes of each discipline, the types of problems each studies, the units of study each employs, the types of end-propositions each desires, and the types of concepts each uses.

CHAPTER II

Perennial Problems of Educational Practice and the Sociopsychological Phenomena Involved with Them

The Meaning of Perennial Problems

The concept of perennial problems, as used here, denotes recurring problems that are more or less inevitable. In the organization and operation of any kind of human enterprise, there are certain matters that inevitably must be faced. That is, decisions about these things have to be made, consciously or unconsciously. For example, in organizing an educational system a decision has to be made as to whether it will enroll only males, only females, or both. This decision is inevitable and can be made according to either a conscious or unconscious policy about whether both sexes should be educated separately or together. At present we have no confirmed knowledge about how the sexes affect one another in terms of the educational process. Consequently, operational policies are based on prejudice, some wisdom, and personal preference. Because agreement does not exist, the problem is one which is likely to be argued for and against over the years. Thus we see that certain problems which are faced by the educational practitioner are inevitable and require him to give some thought as to how he will decide about them. For many of these problems, knowledge will be so inconclusive and preferences so incompatible that only by arbitrary decisions by the authorities of the educational system will actual operation be possible. Because so many of the problems which a practitioner faces have been settled in this way, the same old problems get talked about in the same old argumentative ways each school year—and, very likely, the same old decisions prevail. By the time a practitioner has had ten years of experience, he is so bored with discussion about these matters that he is no longer even willing to talk about them. In this way many of these problems, for which unsatisfactory decisions have been made, continue as an irritating influence upon students and teachers alike and they tend, unfortunately, to become chronic.

The study made of the perennial problems of an educational system has not been enough to provide for either a nomenclature or taxonomy. From observation, experience, and an examination of the agendas of school committees and faculty meetings, however, it is possible to note clusters of similar problems which are the subject of discussion year after year.

The first objective of this section, therefore, will be to identify clusters of similar or seemingly related problems which might be designated perennial problems in the sense that they recur from one school year to the next. The second objective will be to identify the kinds of sociopsychological phenomena that are involved in each of the various clusters of perennial problems. This kind of analysis is the first step in the development of educational sociology as a distinct discipline.

The Different Types of Clusters of Perennial Problems

The first cluster of problems centers around the classroom situation. Ever since it was first asserted that, for economy's sake, one teacher should handle a number of students at a time, teachers have been wrestling with a series of problems involved with the organization and operation of a group of students which came to be termed *the class*. Here are some of these problems:

1. Should the members of the class be of different ages or of the same age?
2. Should the members of the class be of the same sex or of different sexes?
3. Should all members of the class possess the same level or different levels of academic achievement?
4. Should all members of the class possess the same level or different levels of intelligence?
5. Should all members of the class be from similar or different socio-economic, religious, ethnic, or racial backgrounds?
6. How large should a class be? Can varying sizes for different kinds of classes be effectively used?
7. How much responsibility should individual students and classes be given for directing their learning? Should the teacher keep tight or loose control of the class?

8. Should the teacher try to keep the classroom a highly competitive situation, or should he encourage cooperative and supportive relationships between class members?
9. Should the teacher put greater amounts of his energy and time into the instruction of the bright or dull students?
10. Should the teacher be strict or lenient with those students who are having human relations difficulties and are, therefore, unable to carry out the instructional tasks assigned the members of the class?
11. Should the teacher be concerned with character development as well as academic development in the classroom situation?
12. Should the teacher try to raise the life aspirational levels of all students regardless of their chances for fulfilling these aspirations?
13. Should the teachers attempt to control the prestige relationships between students or should he let them develop spontaneously?
14. Should the teacher attempt to suppress classroom conflicts or should he let them evolve if he thinks they will stimulate student participation?
15. Should some class members be given privileges (such as not having to take the final examinations) as rewards for good class performances?
16. Should an instructional plan be maintained whether or not some students seem to be having trouble carrying out the instructional tasks involved?
17. How does one know that one instructional plan or teaching method is better than another?

These are problems that every teacher will face in the classroom situation. Because very little knowledge about these problems has been developed, each teacher tends to evolve his own answers. It is for this reason that most students are anxious to exchange information about teachers and the way they react to these problems.

The second cluster of problems centers about the organization and internal government of the school system. Some of these problems are:

1. In terms of numbers of students and teachers, how large should an educational system be for optimum effectiveness and efficiency?
2. What are the standards of proper behavior for students, teachers, and administrators?
3. To what extent should teachers and students become involved in the various kinds of decision-making that need to be done to administer an educational system effectively?
4. What standards and measures should be used to determine the productivity of an educational system?
5. How should the rewards available within the school system be distributed among the various participants enrolled?

6. By whom and how should human relations problems between teachers, students, and administrators be handled?
7. Should prestige recognitions between the different roles of an educational system be kept as even as possible or should differentiation between them be allowed to develop?
8. What arrangements should be made to make certain that the proper kinds of communications are maintained between the different roles of an educational system?
9. How should the effectiveness of various personnel of an educational system be evaluated?
10. On what bases should responsibility for decision-making be assigned to different roles?
11. What procedures should be used to change organizational arrangements needed to improve the operation of an educational system?

A third cluster of problems centers around attempts to relate an educational system to its clientele. This is often designated *school-community relationships*. Some of these problems are:

1. What kind of decision-making relationships should be established between professional educators and lay boards of education?
2. How should professional educators respond to the various kinds of attacks made against the school system by different groups and organizations of the community?
3. What kinds of relationships should be established between professional educators and parents with respect to providing guidance needed by students?
4. How should the professional organizations to which educators belong relate to governmental authorities with respect to such matters as obtaining adequate support for educational systems and for developing the proper kinds of working conditions?
5. How should professional educators relate to the political organizations of the community?
6. Should professional educators attempt to take leadership positions in dealing with community problems?
7. Should professional educators assume some responsibility for developing educational policies for the community, or should they consider themselves only the educational "machinery" for implementing policies formulated by the citizenry?

A fourth cluster of problems centers around the development and achievement of individuals. Some of these problems are:

1. What effect does the general psychological atmosphere or climate of an educational system have upon the individual development of students, teachers, and administrators?

2. What effect does living in a particular community setting have upon the individual development of students and teachers?
3. Should educational practitioners focus primarily upon the academic achievement of students or should they assume responsibility for all aspects of individual development?
4. Should educational practitioners assume responsibility for the intellectual achievement of those students who don't care about or who resist this kind of development?
5. Should teachers endeavor to bring about intellectual development which is incompatible with the learning that students have acquired from other community organizations and their families?
6. What theory of learning most accurately describes the way new behaviors are acquired? Is remedial, corrective, and rehabilitative instruction a responsibility of the teacher who is primarily assigned to classes organized for advanced academic work?
7. What are the proper points in an individual's life at which to introduce certain kinds of learning?
8. Are certain course sequences or prerequisites essential to proper intellectual development?
9. How does the student bring about an integration between the disparate kinds of development that result from schooling?
10. Is development under coercive psychological conditions the same as that under voluntary conditions?
11. How much responsibility should the student assume for his own development?
12. Should the teacher expect to bring about maximum development in all areas of human development or is there an optimum level that should be sought?
13. How much learning in different areas of development should be expected and worked for?

A fifth cluster of problems centers around the part that educational systems and educator should play in a society. Some of these problems are:

1. Should an educational system tend to focus the attention and behaviors of the people in the society upon change and the development of new institutions, or upon the preservation of old and tested institutions?
2. What responsibilities do teachers have with respect to analyzing, criticizing, and attempting to improve the society?
3. Should teachers organize the curriculum of an educational system around actual materials drawn from the society, or should it use fictional and nonfictional materials drawn from any society, real or imaginary? Should the curriculum content be provincial and

nonfictional, or should it be cosmopolitan and include both fictional and nonfictional material?

4. In what kinds of people and roles should the authority for formulating the objectives of an educational system rest?
5. Should the curriculums of educational systems be organized so as to deal with the immediate societal problems, or should it be organized primarily in terms of readying people to live in an improved society—whether or not such a society exists in the present? In brief, are curriculums to be designed in terms of the present society, or for some kind of society which—it is hoped—will come into being?
6. Should the educational system and its curriculums be organized so as to make clear to all members of the society how the society is organized, and how it works, or is this kind of curriculum to be reserved for a certain elite?
7. Should the curriculums of an educational system be organized so as to give training in the various disciplines as disciplines, or should it be organized so as to utilize the disciplines as instrumental means for analyzing the society and its problems, and for developing ways to bring about social change?
8. Should the curriculums of educational systems differentiate between different social classes of the society?
9. Should the curriculums of educational systems focus primarily on the problems of social management of the society, or upon the learning of specific intellectual and vocational skills?

Each of the problems contained in these five types of clusters needs to be investigated by the educational practitioner in three different ways. He must determine which of a number of action alternatives should be chosen as the "proper" or "right" one to follow, what kind of action has to be taken to implement the chosen alternative effectively, and how best to institute and manage the kind of conditions and actions required to implement the chosen alternative effectively.

The questions contained in each of the identified clusters do not represent all the perennial questions or problems that educational practitioners face. It is not the purpose of this book to develop an inclusive inventory of all these problems, but merely to point out that such problems exist and that they are the ones for which the educational practitioner needs knowledge if he is to do more than handle them in an intuitive, personalized way. Furthermore, as has been previously stated, they are the starting point for the educational sociologist in his efforts to contribute to the development of the kinds of knowledge needed by the educational practitioner.

Types of Sociopsychological Phenomena to be Coordinated with the Clusters of Perennial Problems

Once clusters of perennial problems faced by the educational practitioner have been identified, along with illustrative kinds of questions contained in each, it becomes possible for the educational sociologist to make the first kind of contribution which the educational practitioner, by himself, cannot. This has to do with connecting the perennial problems with the kinds of sociopsychological phenomena that seem to be common to each of the clusters. That is, it becomes possible to perceive that the questions contained under the different clusters are essentially questions about different aspects of the same kind of sociopsychological phenomena. The practiced eye of the educational sociologist can quickly perceive that two seemingly different questions actually pertain to the same kind of sociopsychological phenomena. When this is perceived, it then becomes possible to make use of existing sociopsychological theory and research findings, research technology, and generalizations that have been gradually developed about this kind of phenomena over the years. It is this kind of systematic connection between the physical sciences and engineering, for example, that has made possible the rapid advancement of engineering during the last century. It is this systematic connection between the biological and chemical sciences and the field of medicine that has given the medicine its great forward thrust during the last fifty years.

To provide an illustration pertinent to educational practice, the first cluster of perennial problems will be utilized. It was asserted that every teacher who has been or is involved in conducting a classroom group must face the problems included in this cluster. The teacher can deal with these problems consciously or unconsciously, but every teacher must evolve a set of principles, techniques, and policies concerning them. At present, each teacher does the best he can: some are quite successful, others are not. The concern of educational administrators and scientists with these problems has led to countless research studies on the characteristics of the "good" teacher. After some forty years of such studies, the main conclusions that have been developed are that "good" teachers have different characteristics, and so do "bad" teachers. This has been most discouraging to these investigators. The point to be made is that these researchers and administrators were investigating the wrong kind of phenomena and, as a result, had posed and formulated the wrong kinds of research problems.

After examining the questions in the cluster pertaining to the classroom situation, the educational sociologist would say that they concern sociopsychological phenomena involving small or face-to-face groups. Whether or not a teacher would be successful or effective with a classroom group depends not so much upon his peculiar or unique personality traits as upon his ability to understand, to analyze, and to take effective and efficient action with a face-to-face group. His unique or peculiar personality characteristics matter little if the teacher lacked the knowledge to understand and analyze the face-to-face group and/or the skill to take effective action with it. Under these conditions, there is a strong likelihood that the class would prove to be a poor one and that the teaching would be poor too. The phenomena of small or face-to-face groups could be utilized by the educational practitioner to develop good teaching and effective answers to perennial problems of this kind. The existing knowledge that has been developed by the field of sociology in this area could be used to develop new knowledge usable by educational practitioners, and to aid in the planning of research that the educational sociologist must ultimately conduct to investigate problems about which no knowledge exists at present. (More extensive discussion of knowledge development and research planning procedures will be provided in Chapters III and IV.)

Small or face-to-face groups may be described as social units which consist of a number of interdependent individuals whose behavior is regulated and coordinated by a set of standards that have been learned and are held in common. An examination of that area of sociology that investigates small groups indicates that they evolve a social structure, a set of internal interactions or dynamics, and a set of rules or norms that constitute the culture of the group and which, when learned by the members of the group, enable them to live and take action together. Sociopsychological phenomena of this kind pertain to the cluster of problems that center around the classroom situation. To deal with such a question as "Should the teacher try to keep the classroom a highly competitive situation or should cooperative and supportive relationships between classroom members be encouraged?" requires an analysis and utilization of small or face-to-face group knowledge.

This question, of course, as a perennial problem, has to be considered in three different ways: What is the right or proper thing to do? What, in light of existing conditions, must be done to carry out the chosen line of action? What are the best ways for doing what has to be done to effectively implement the chosen alternative? Although answers to each of these questions must be evolved before effective action can be taken, it must be recognized, that—regardless of which dimension is being considered at any given time—answers to each of the questions will require the utilization of knowledge about the pertinent sociopsychological phenomena.

One aspect of face-to-face groups that has been examined involves the effect that the social characteristics (e.g., age, sex, and socioeconomic backgrounds) of group members have upon the development and operation of the group. A number of the questions included in the cluster of perennial problems centering around the classroom situation pertained to the social characteristics of class members: Should the members of the class be of different ages or the same age? Should the members of the class be of similar or different socioeconomic backgrounds?

A review of books on the theory and research of small or face-to-face groups will identify numerous group factors that have been studied to determine their effect upon group behavior and operation. Although not all of these will prove relevant to the perennial problems involved in the classroom situation, many of them will. Such topics as social power or influence relationships between group members, leadership behavior, the development or formation of group standards, group productivity, group problem-solving, the effect of group operation on individual achievement, prestige relationships between members, socioemotional aspects of group life, group conflict and cooperation, informal or friendship relationships among group members, group goal-setting, group task-planning, the effects of group size upon group operations, and authority relationships among group members suggest strongly that the kinds of perennial problems encountered in the classroom situation need to be identified and connected with small or face-to-face group phenomena. When this is done, the chances of studying the right kind of phenomena as a means of obtaining answers to these different perennial problems will be greatly increased.

Next, an effort will be made to identify the kind of sociopsychological phenomena to which the second cluster of perennial problems should be connected. This cluster, it will be remembered, involves perennial problems that center about difficulties with organizational patterns or designs and the internal government of educational systems. As the educational sociologist reviews the kinds of perennial problems found in this cluster, he will most certainly suggest that they involve formal organization phenomena.

In their book on *Formal Organizations,* Blau and Scott designate formal organizations as "organizations that have been deliberately established for a certain purpose. If the accomplishment of an objective requires collective effort, men set up an organization designed to coordinate the activities of many persons and to furnish incentives for others to join them for this purpose."[1] After providing an example of this type of human organization, Blau and Scott point out that the goals to be attained, the rules by which the behavior of the members of the organization is governed, and the structural relationships between roles as defined by the organizational charts "have been consciously designed *a priori* to anticipate and guide interaction and activities."

In discussing educational systems as formal organizations, Jensen and Goodson state that a school system is comprised of a network of roles that express expectations about the rights and obligations of the persons who occupy these roles (such as students, teachers, service personnel, administrators, public representatives, and sometimes parents).[2] This system of interacting roles and groups is structured and designed with the aim of accomplishing the educational tasks required to fulfill the educational needs of the society that supports it.

When the various perennial problems included in this cluster are

---

[1] Peter M. Blau and W. Richard Scott, *Formal Organizations* (San Francisco: Chandler Publishing Company, 1962), p. 5.

[2] Gale E. Jensen and Max R. Goodson, *The Formal Organization of School Systems* (Ann Arbor, Mich.: Ann Arbor Publishers, 1956), pp. 10–11.

reviewed, it is not difficult to perceive the connection between them and the kind of sociopsychological phenomena incorporated in the foregoing definitions of formal organizations. Such questions as "What should be the standards of proper behavior for students, teachers, and administrators?" and "What standards and measures should be used to determine the productivity of an educational system?" clearly become perennial problems that should be perceived as and formulated in terms of formal organization phenomena. When they are conceived in this fashion, the probability of formulating the right kind of research problem is increased.

The range of formal organization phenomena that have been considered by sociologists as relevant to the study of formal organizations is rather extensive. Topical study areas to be found in the literature include bureaucracy, productivity, decision-making, communication patterns, role conflict, role definition and perception, organizational security, influence and power relationships between roles, succession from one leader to another, organizational innovation and change, hierarchy, organizational authority patterns, informal and clique relationships, organizational morale and apathy, absenteeism and turnover, administrative and managerial behavior, optimum size, incentive systems, line-and-staff relationships, role analysis, and organization prestige. Each of the problems listed under the second cluster is related to one or more of the different topical areas identified as formal organization phenomena. In light of this relationship, it is rather interesting to note that these problems of educational practice were not investigated as formal organization phenomena until very recently.

The third cluster of perennial problems involved school-community relations. An examination by an educational sociologist of these problems probably would result in a statement that they involve "community" phenomena. He probably would indicate further that, although sociologists have great difficulty in providing a formal definition for such phenomena, they recognize that these are a generic kind of phenomena and subject to study as such. Reiss, in *A Review and Evaluation of Research on Community,* points out that for the period 1949–52 approximately two fifths of the articles in four prominent sociological periodicals were focused upon the community.[3] The difficulty of providing a formal definition for community phenomena is to be seen also in the publication *Community and Adult Education,* which attempts to explore and define the relationships between the organization and operation of human communities and the part that adult education plays in the maintenance, reorganization, and improvement of human communities.[4] Both the authors of this publication and Reiss recognize that human communities incorporate sociological and psychological elements and that the problems of definition is one of discovering the distinctive or generic features of the combination of elements that constitute community phenomena.

A simple definition of these phenomena is that human communities are comprised of sets of individuals, groups, and formal organizations which have become interconnected and unified in ways designed to fulfill thc basic needs and life aspirations of the people contained in them. Within this community structure, there evolves a characteristic set of interactions and behavioral norms that shape the personalities of the people that comprise the community. The people, in turn, consciously or unconsciously revamp the structured interconnections, interactions, and norms from time to time and thus bring about social changes in the community.

A review of the perennial problems in the school-community relationships cluster enables one to perceive quite readily that such questions as "How should professional educators relate to the political organizations of the community?" and "Should professional educators attempt to take leadership positions in dealing with problems of the community?" involve community phenomena. This means that perennial problems of this kind clearly should be conceptualized and investigated in terms of such phenomena. To do otherwise would be to study and obtain findings about phenomena which were not relevant, or only indirectly related, to problems of this kind.

These assertions are further supported when one reviews the kinds of study topics that are incorporated in the sociological study of human communities. These include the study of demographic or population trends of communities; the ecological characteristics of

[3] Albert J. Reiss, Jr., "A Review and Evaluation of Research on Community." An unpublished memorandum prepared for the Committee on Social Behavior of the Social Science Research Council, Nashville, Tennessee, 1954.

[4] Wilbur C. Hallenbeck, *et al., Community and Adult Education* (Chicago: Adult Education Association of the United States, 1962).

communities; the behavior of masses and crowds; the flow of information within and between communities; influence relationships between individuals, groups, and formal organizations; problems of social change and reorganization; community political systems; the sociopsychological processes of interaction, assimilation, diffusion, innovation, isolation, competition, cooperation, conflict, disorganization, and alienation; the social stratification and differentiation of communities; occupational profiles and social mobility in communities; the effects of the institutions of a society upon its communities; and such social problems as delinquency, crime, mental illness, dependency and welfare difficulties, and suicide; and intergroup problems involving racial, ethnic, and religious relationships. These subject matter topics more than cover the sample of perennial problems pertaining to school-community relations. To date we have been able to develop only a few descriptive accounts or books about these problems. The development of knowledge that would be useful to the educational practitioner is sadly lacking. Failure to connect these problems to these kinds of sociopsychological phenomena has led to the failure to develop any systematic research, theory, and the eventual formulation of knowledge which could have some effect upon educational practice.

The fourth cluster of perennial problems involved the development and achievement problems of individuals. Probably none of the different kinds of perennial problems listed herein is so intimately troublesome to the educational practitioner as the problems contained in this cluster. It is interesting to note, however, that it is in this area that the educational practitioner is most skillful in perceiving the kinds of developmental change and achievements that are taking place in people. Seldom, however, is he certain as to what produces these changes or whether they are of the right kind. As a result, educational practitioners reward and punish individual students pretty much in terms of their personal beliefs, values, and skills. Very often this kind of behavior on the part of the educational practitioner cannot be understood, and is most often misunderstood, by the students. In such cases, the individual development and achievement creates behavior patterns and traits that lead to trouble for both the individual and his society.

An examination by the educational sociologist of the various perennial problems contained in this cluster will probably result in his identifying the types of sociopsychological phenomena involved as those of personality development and social learning. Such problems as "What effect does the general psychological atmosphere or climate of an educational system have upon the development and learning of students, teachers, and administrators?" and "What effect does living in a particular community setting have upon the learning and development of students?" would be identified by the educational sociologist as problems involving sociopsychological phenomena of personality development and social learning.[5] Others might identify them as phenomena of personality socialization.[6]

A fairly simple definition of these types of sociopsychological phenomena is that they pertain to the processes through which an individual acquires the behavioral adaptations that enable him to take the kinds of actions required for him to fulfill his various needs and wants in a specified kind of social environment—an environment which requires that needs-meeting activities on the part of individuals be consistent with the rules or norms of the community or society. In brief, these phenomena refer to the processes by which individuals learn the behaviors required by their community and society. It is only by "learning" their social environment that individuals are able to engage in successful needs-meeting behavior. It is in the process of "learning" their social environment that personality socialization takes place. As Jensen states in a work on community reorganization and community development:

> . . . the members of the community *must learn* consciously and/or unconsciously the particular set of human relationships interactions, and behavioral standards on which the particular organizational form of their community rests and by which living in the community is directed and controlled. It is by this *educational process* that the members of a community literally build into their personal character the underlying and basic sociopsychological characteristics of the prevailing forms of community organization.[7]

Study topics to be found in connection with these phenomena include such things as motivation, needs, intelligence, achievement,

[5] Neil J. Smelser and William T. Smelser, *Personality and Social Systems* (New York: John Wiley & Sons, Inc., 1963), Chap. 3; Logan Wilson and William L. Kolb, *Sociological Analysis* (New York: Harcourt, Brace & World, Inc., 1949), Part II, pp. 155–57.

[6] Wilson and Kolb, *op. cit.*

[7] Gale Jensen, *Community Reorganization for Economic Development: The Sociopsychological and Educational Bases of Economic Development in Human Communities* (from material for a forthcoming publication).

social perception, the acquisition of values, feelings and emotions, the biological and physiological bases of personality development and human learning, aspirational levels, the acquisition of skills and habits, human drives and instincts, forms of personality disorganization and deviation, thinking and problem-solving behavior, concept formation, defense mechanisms and behavior, prejudice, the effects of different kinds and amounts of reward and punishment upon the kind and rate of social learning, individual learning under different types of authority and leadership, and the human life cycle. The connection between theory and research centering around these kinds of topics and the perennial problems listed under the cluster of individual development and achievement is relatively easy to perceive for the educational sociologist. To the extent that future theory development and research related to these kinds of perennial problems can be coordinated with personality development and social learning phenomena, the probabilities of formulating knowledge that will be useful to the educational practitioner for dealing with these kinds of perennial problems will be increased.

The fifth cluster of perennial problems centered around the part or role that educational systems and educators should play in a society. These problems pertain to important questions of social policy that affect the long-range development of the society. These are problems which, generally speaking, educators have been somewhat hesitant to attack directly because they are highly controversial and because they are problems to which the most powerful individuals, groups, and organizations of a society are most sensitive. An examination by the educational sociologist of the problems included in this cluster would probably lead him to say that the sociopsychological phenomena inherent to these problems are those involving societal institutions.

A simple definition of societal institutions is that they are the social mechanisms and rules by which the activities of human beings are ordered so as to enable individuals to live and achieve according to the values they have acquired from the culture of the society and to assure that the basic functional needs of the society itself are met.[8] Briefly stated, the functions of societal institutions are to pro-

---

[8] Wilson and Kolb, *op. cit.*, Part V, pp. 513–16; Bernard Berelson and Gary A. Steiner, *Human Behavior: An Inventory of Scientific Findings.* (New York. Harcourt, Brace & World, Inc., 1964), Chap. 10, pp. 383–84.

vide for the survival of the society and to provide orderly and prescribed ways for individuals to engage in activities designed to meet their personal needs. Every society evolves a set of these institutions. In some societies the religious institutions may dominate; in others, the dominant institutions may be political, military, or economic in nature.

It is relatively easy to recognize that such perennial problems as "Should educational systems tend to focus the attention and behaviors of the people of the society upon change and the development of new institutions or upon the preservation of old and tested institutions?" and "What responsibilities do teachers have with respect to analyzing, criticizing, and attempting to improve the society?" are intimately involved with societal institutions phenomena. Relevant study topics include such things as industrialization, technology, economic motivation and development, problems of unemployment, the labor force, employer-employee relations, the occupational structure of the society, political parties, governments and political systems, political participation, political preferences, education, academic freedom, the social attitudes of educators, the social status and social-class characteristics of educators, the social effects of changing military technology, the relationships of civilian and military roles and personnel, religious sects and organizations, the effects of social changes upon the family, the religious affiliation and attitudes of governmental leaders, political and economic philosophies, the value systems that dominate different institutions, and the role of the courts and lawyers in maintaining an orderly society.

Prospects for improving knowledge usable by the educational practitioner for dealing with perennial problems pertaining to the role of educational systems and educators in society depend largely upon the ability of the educational sociologist to incorporate and utilize societal phenomena in theory and research ventures aimed at the development of more adequate knowledge for coping with these kinds of perennial problems. This is something that the educational practitioner is unable to do for himself. It is something that other kinds of sociologists are likely to do only incidentally, and perhaps even accidentally. It is this special kind of role that the educational sociologist must fill if societal phenomena are to be connected to these kinds of perennial problems in a profitable way. Improved knowledge relevant to these perennial problems has been slow to develop because of the failure to institute and organize the educational sociologists' role. When the field of professional education fully understands and accepts these relationships, it will become possible to make some advances in educational practice.

The Significance of Coordinating Perennial Problems with Sociopsychological Phenomena

The significance of being able to identify the kind of sociopsychological phenomena involved with different kinds of perennial problems can be easily and clearly seen in the formulation of a research problem. The example given below is the actual product of one graduate student's efforts to formulate a problem for his dissertation.

> I am a Latin teacher with three years of experience. I teach in a church-society high school of 1300 students. Our constituency is of of the middle and upper-middle socioeconomic level and places quite a strong emphasis on college education. For this reason, a very large percentage of our students follow a college preparatory sequence, and better than 60 per cent of these college-bound students take Latin. The strong emphasis on college entrance results in students of widely varied ability taking our Latin courses. Three years ago it was decided to "skim off" the very bright students and place them in an honors class in Latin. Because I have the largest amount of Latin preparation of any of the four full-time Latin teachers, I was assigned to teach these honors classes on both the first- and second-year levels of study. I was assigned also to teach an advanced third-year course which has a "B" grade prerequisite, and hence is almost another honors class.
>
> Because I have been teaching for such a relatively short time, there are many problems which face me as I carry on the normal duties of teaching. When I was assigned these special classes, I really was beset with problems. In addition to the regular questions a young teacher has concerning his classes, the teaching of these honors classes really put me in the "soup." Do I treat these as a special group? If so, should I do it both academically and socially, just academically, just socially, or what? If I do treat them in a special way academically, and/or socially, will the added recognition spur them on to greater development, or will it tend to result in "swelled heads"? Should I use the same textual material and just be more precise in my requirements, or should I use the same material and hope that the added competition will arouse them to a greater effort? Should I use the same material and then evaluate them on the classes' achievement, or should I use completely different mate-

rials and then evaluate them accordingly? What is the philosophy behind the establishment of these honors classes? What are we trying to achieve? What is our aim? What end-products are we looking for? The problems facing me seem to center about discovering the rationale behind the establishment of these honors classes, the best methods by which they can be taught, and the manner in which they should be evaluated.

The description provided by this young teacher of his experience in his educational system is familiar to every experienced educational practitioner. The next section of the proposal states a number of questions for which our erstwhile researcher-practitioner would like to have answers:

1. What is the rationale of the school system for the formation of this homogeneous group?
2. What are the social advantages or disadvantages of this grouping for the students involved?
3. What are the psychological advantages or disadvantages of this grouping for the students involved?
4. What are the academic advantages or disadvantages of this grouping for the students involved?
5. What are the social advantages or disadvantages for the students not involved in this grouping?
6. What are the psychological advantages or disadvantages of students not involved in this grouping?
7. What are the academic advantages or disadvantages for the students not involved in this grouping?
8. What types of benefits are we seeking by engaging in this grouping?
9. Do the positive effects of this grouping outweigh the negative aspects with regard to the later development of the students?
10. Should the homogeneous group be taught special subject matter?
11. Should the homogeneous group be taught with a different psychological technique—i. e., a different teacher-class relationship?
12. How should a homogeneous group be evaluated?
13. Should a homogeneous group be evaluated at all?
14. What is the attitude of other schools towards homogeneous grouping? If they have such groups, what is their philosophy? Their present practice regarding materials and evaluation?
15. How does membership in such a group affect later performance in the same subject-matter area?

These questions will be recognized quickly as the perennial problems of the educational practitioner. The crucial matter at this point is: What kinds of sociopsychological phenomena have to be investigated to obtain the right kind of research findings—the kind that make possible the development of knowledge usable by the educational practitioner? In the third section of his proposal, this graduate student made use of his social science training to identify the kinds of sociopsychological phenomena he thought were indigenous to the different kinds of questions he had raised and, therefore, the kinds of phenomena that needed to be investigated.

Questions 3, 6, and 15 were identified as problems which required the study of personality development and social learning. Questions 2, 4, 5, 7, 10, 11, and 12 were designated as problems which required the investigation of small or face-to-face group phenomena. Questions 1, 8, 9, and 14 were deemed to be problems which would require the investigation of formal organization phenomena. In addition, it was asserted that some of these questions could be perceived as involving more than one type of sociopsychological phenomena. For example, Questions 8 and 9 might be investigated as community phenomena as well as formal organization phenomena, and question 4 might be studied as formal organization phenomena as well as small group phenomena.

This connecting of different types of sociopsychological phenomena to the different kinds of perennial problems is of the greatest significance. Specifically, the establishment of a connection between these two concepts make possible the formulation of research problems and problems of practice with concepts that theoretically represent or refer to the phenomena involved. One cannot successfully investigate a perennial question which requires the study of small group phenomena by investigating community phenomena. When one identifies the kind of phenomena that is inherent in a perennial problem, it becomes possible in both practice and research to work with concepts that in fact pertain to those phenomena. What often happens is that problems which pertain to one kind of phenomena are unconsciously formulated with concepts that pertain to a different kind of phenomena. The connecting of a perennial problem to a specific kind or kinds of phenomena leads to the selection of concepts that in fact pertain to the phenomena involved.

In the fourth section of the research proposal, theory for the different types of phenomena is identified and, from this theory, concepts are chosen which the author believes to be the specific kinds of factors that pertain to the different perennial problems. For example, the author identified Questions 2, 3, 5, 6, and 11 as the most central to the practical difficulties he was encountering. As will be remembered, he had asserted that the kinds of phenomena involved with Question 2 were small group phenomena. To utilize the proper concepts for formulating his research problem, he reviewed the existing theory and conceptual frameworks pertaining to human groups and then was able to pinpoint a set of concepts which he felt bore directly, and specifically, on the groups factors that pertain to the practical difficulties he had to analyze and for which he had to make action decisions. These theoretical concepts were personal prestige, privilege, problem-solving, and friendship. If he used these concepts for formulating his research problem, according to the formal theoretical definitions that have been attached to them, he was reasonably certain that he would be investigating the "right" kind of things.

He also felt that Question 3 was central to his situation. This kind of problem he had connected with personality development and social learning. Taking advantage of existing theory about these phenomena, he was able to locate a set of concepts that he felt was directly related to the difficulties he encountered in his practice situation. These concepts were gratification-deprivation balance, need for peer approval, need for self-expressive activity, and need for affection. These concepts, he felt certain, would enable him to investigate the proper kinds of phenomena so long as Question 3 represented the kind of perennial problem about which he wished to develop new knowledge.

In this way, a rather extensive list of concepts for formulating a research problem was developed. All these the author judged to be related in some way to the kinds of perennial problems he had identified as being central to his practice situation. He utilized these concepts to formulate a number of research problems. Then he made a general statement of the one he finally chose to explore further in terms of possible research approaches and methodology:

> Do personal-prestige relationships in a homogeneous classroom group affect the gratification of the peer-approval needs of students in ways that affect the group problem-solving participation of student members?

It can be seen that this statement contains concepts which pertain to two kinds of sociopsychological phenomena, viz., personality development and small groups. With this kind of problem formulation, a researcher always knows what it is that he is trying to study. The coordination of different types of sociopsychological phenomena with the different types of perennial problems that educational practitioners encounter goes a long way towards providing a way for knowing *what* is to be studied.

Summary

This chapter provided an analysis of the perennial problems with which educational practitioners are confronted and an identification of the kinds of sociopsychological phenomena associated with them. An effort was made to identify the groups or clusters of problems that center around different educational situations. The first cluster of problems centered around the classroom situation. The second cluster involved the organization and internal government of educational systems. The third cluster pertained to the relationships between an educational system and its community or clientele. The fourth cluster was comprised of perennial problems concerning the personal development and achievement of students and teachers. The fifth cluster consisted of problems of determining the roles that educational systems and educators should play in a society. These clusters of problems provide the starting points for the kind of development of educational sociology that can effectively contribute to the work of the educational practitioner.

If an educational sociologist is to contribute to an understanding of these perennial problems, he must perceive clearly the kinds of sociopsychological phenomena that are involved in each of the clusters. If he is to develop usable knowledge for dealing with the problems contained in each of the clusters, he must make certain that he is investigating the kinds of phenomena that are indigenous to these problems.

CHAPTER III

Knowledge-Development Procedures in Educational Sociology

The primary task of educational sociology is that of developing knowledge that can be used as the conceptual bases for those phases of educational practice which involve the management of sociological and sociopsychological variables. This system of knowledge, therefore, must be organized in a fashion that makes possible effective action-taking for coping with the problems with which the educational practitioner is confronted.

The job of developing this kind of knowledge is concerned with defining and ordering concepts so as to create new forms of knowledge organization that will make possible improved practical control over those variables the educational practitioner utilizes in achieving a specified set of educational outcomes. The primary need of the educational practitioner is to be equal to the action problems which continuously confront him and gradually to develop greater control over them. Thus, although educational sociological knowledge is as theoretical in character as any other kind of sociological knowledge, its formulation is heavily influenced by the pragmatic orientation of the practitioner. This does not mean that the educational sociologist will not be as much interested in validating his theoretical system as any other sociologist; rather, it means that—because he is greatly influenced by the needs of the educational practitioner—he does it in a somewhat different way. He must first create and evaluate a system of theory in terms of its immediate power to deal with problems of practice and, secondly, give attention to its logical consistency and empirical testing.[1] Other sociologists usually state their objectives in reverse order and may very often not be much concerned about whether their theory and research will produce anything of use for educational practice.

[1] Indirectly, of course, he tests and validates his theory through observing what happens when the educational practitioner attempts to utilize his theory in dealing with practical situations.

Borrowing from Related Behavioral Sciences

When the situation in which the educational practitioner has to take action is examined, it is not difficult to understand why he has to organize the conceptual bases of his action in such a way as to put a utilitarian emphasis on the organizational pattern of this knowledge. There are a number of identifiable characteristics which are common to these situations. First, the educational practitioner is supposed to make possible the achievement of certain specified educational objectives or outcomes. Second, he is supposed to be able to overcome the various kinds of perplexities and operational problems that may be encountered in achieving these educational objectives. Third, he is expected to utilize his specialized knowledges and skills to analyze or diagnose the problematical situation and identify the conditions which are creating difficulties for those persons and groups supporting his work. Fourth, he is expected to devise plans of action which provide for the educational needs of his supporters. Fifth, he is expected to know how to implement selected plans in an effective and efficient way.

The task of borrowing and reformulating the knowledge of another discipline is never easy. Very often the knowledge developed by other disciplines is not pertinent to educational practice. Also, it often happens that the investigations of other disciplines are so narrow and artificial that the findings have no potential for application. It is only by extensively sifting through the existing theory and research of other areas of sociological investigation that the educational sociologist is likely to locate some theory which has pertinence for the problems of educational practice. Whenever he is able to identify theory and research of this kind, it becomes possible to borrow from another discipline.

The initial step, then, is that of screening the theory and research of the different areas of sociology to identify the existing theory and the research findings which in some way appear to be relevant to the problem of educational practice. To determine which knowledge is relevant, however, one must first identify a particular problem of practice and the kinds of phenomena inherent in it. Then one must make certain that the phenomena contained in the problem are of the same kind as those contained in the theory and research findings.

Once this has been accomplished, it becomes possible to move to the next step.

The second step involves a conceptual reorganization which requires connecting important or central sociological concepts with the conceptual indices the educational practitioner uses to direct or guide his action. In brief, it is necessary to link theoretical concepts from sociology with certain overt symptoms or empirical signs present in a practice situation. The practitioner is sensitive to these signs and uses them to decide whether his efforts to deal with an educational problem are going well or not. The detection of these symptoms, or signs, has been learned through the practitioner's observation of the activities and behaviors of persons involved in educational programs. Specifically, they are signs which (as he has learned from past experience) indicate (1) whether satisfactory progress is being made with respect to achieving given educational objectives; (2) whether the persons involved in the program are "pulling together" to the degree necessary for effective and efficient implementation of instructional activities; (3) whether individual members are participating in the most effective way; (4) whether individual members show signs of satisfaction or dissatisfaction with their experience in the program; (5) whether individual members are developing behaviors specified by the instructional objectives guiding the venture. In other words, the educational practitioner has learned from past experience that these five things are critical in determining whether a particular educational venture will be successful. He, therefore, employs them as operational indices for judging how well his program is going. He intuitively collects evidence that will demonstrate whether these particular operational indices are at the level they should be to insure a successful educational venture. When he judges them to be at a satisfactory level, he will indicate that the program will be likely to produce the desired educational outcomes. When he discovers that some of them are not operating in ways conducive to the attainment of the specified instructional or educational objectives, he will take steps to correct or change them.

In the screening of sociological knowledge to identify concepts which might be profitably coordinated with the operational indices utilized by the educational practitioner, it is important to choose with discrimination and skill those ideas that are to be used for conceptualizing the phenomena involved in educational practice. Typically, there is a wide range of concepts available for coordination with the operational indices. The choice of one set of concepts rather than another has definite implications for the way the educational practitioner will analyze and respond to the practice situation. It is quite possible for one set of ideas to be more effective than another; thus the one chosen and learned by the educational practitioner will determine how effective he will be in practice situations.

The coordination of theoretical concepts from the different areas of sociology with the empirical signs or symptoms associated with the five operational indices increases the ability of the educational practitioner to analyze the conditions which influence and produce these indices because it now becomes possible to use theory and research to identify other kinds of variables that affect them. The five operational indices can be conceived of as dependent variables which are influenced by and related to different variables identified by the various areas of sociological investigation. When the logical connections between these variables and the operational indices become better understood, the educational practitioner may more clearly determine how these variables affect the operational indices with which he is concerned. This makes possible a more refined conceptualization of the phenomena which operate in practice situations.

When carrying out action to fulfill the educational needs of communities which create and support an educational system, educational practitioners soon learn that sociopsychological phenomena are centrally involved in almost everything they do. Whether educational practitioners are working with instructional groups, athletic teams, committees, clubs, departmental groups, administrative groups, or any of the other numerous formal and informal groups found in an educational system, the sociopsychological variables present in each of these situations will greatly influence the outcomes of their efforts. In the following material which is designed to provide specific examples of how the borrowing and translation process works, instructional group and formal organization problems which the educational practitioner encounters will be utilized to demonstrate this process. An example of reformulating sociological knowledge for coping with instructional group problems is provided first.

After identifying specific problems of instructional group practice, it is necessary for the educational sociologist to locate and categorize sociopsychological theories and research findings as the initial step in identifying whatever theory and research appears to be inherent in the problems. The discipline of social psychology, one general area of sociological investigation, studies such phenomena as human groups, formal organizations, the social organization of human communities, and the sociopsychological aspects of human learning and personality formation. Some of the theory and research in social psychology is likely to be relevant to instructional groups situations; some not. From first examination it is quite certain that the investigation of human groups by social psychology is relevant to problems of educational practice as found in instructional group situations. It is quite possible that the other areas which social psychology investigates would also develop knowledge relevant to problems of instructional groups. So as not to make our task too burdensome, however, let us limit ourselves to social psychological knowledge about human groups. It is this set of theory and research findings that is most obviously likely to contain some significant ideas and operational implications for the way the educational practitioner should analyze and control sociopsychological variables inherent in instructional group situations.

The next step for the educational sociologist is to coordinate theoretical concepts about human groups with the overt symptoms and empirical signs generated in instructional groups—the signs which the educational practitioner uses to decide whether a particular group is or is not doing well. These signs, as was previously noted, are utilized as operational indices to judge whether the group is doing well. Specifically, the educational practitioner uses these indices to collect evidence on (1) the progress the group is making towards achieving the instructional objectives, (2) how well it is carrying out the instructional tasks being used to achieve the objectives, (3) how well individual members are contributing to the instructional tasks, (4) the degree of satisfaction with their group experience individual members are evidencing, and (5) how well individual members are learning the behaviors specified by the instructional objectives.

By utilizing concepts from social psychology about human groups, the educational practitioner may coordinate theoretical concepts with the empirical signs or symptoms of these five operational indices. For example, the concepts of group productivity and group achievement, formulated to investigate the theoretical and research problems of social psychologists, pertain as well to the educational practitioner's concern about class or group progress toward instructional objectives.[2] The educational practitioner can employ the concept of group cohesiveness to observe and analyze problems concerning the ability of the group to maintain itself as a group.[3] Similarly, the concept of attraction can be employed to examine the involvement and satisfaction of individual members with their experience in the group.[4] The concept of group problem-solving functions can be used to assess the effectiveness of the participation by individual members.[5] The concept of behavioral integration or outcomes can be used to examine the achievement of individuals with respect to acquiring the behaviors set forth in the instructional objectives.[6]

The coordination of sociopsychological concepts with the empirical signs associated with the five operational indices increases the ability of the educational practitioner to analyze the conditions which influence and produce these indices. He can now use theory and research findings to identfy other group factors or variables that affect these five operational indices. These indices can be perceived as variables influenced by and related to various sociopsychological variables of human groups. When the educational practitioner grasps the logical connections between group variables and the operational indices, he is better able to understand how the group variables can "cause" the operational indices, which he continuously observes, to fluctuate the way they do. This makes possible a refined and selected conceptualization of group phenomena involved in instructional work. For example, in attempting to identify more specifically the variables which affect the five operational indices, the concepts of group structure, authority relations, group norms, power relationships, emotional modalities, group culture, and conflict dynamics

---

[2] Ralph H. Stogdill, *Individual Behavior and Group Achievement* (New York: Oxford University Press, Inc., 1959), Chap. 6.

[3] Dorwin Cartwright and Alvin Zander (eds.), *Group Dynamics and Theory* (New York: Harper & Row, Publishers, 1960), Part II.

[4] Stogdill, *op. cit.*

[5] Paul A. Hare (ed.), *Handbook of Small Group Research* (New York: The Free Press of Glencoe, 1962), pp. 66–70.

[6] Stogdill, *op. cit.*, Chaps. 5 and 6.

are introduced.[7] These conceptual categories make it possible to perceive more accurately and microscopically the kinds of variables which produce the changes that appear in the operational indices. It is these conceptual categories that serve as the basis for theoretical and research work about human groups. They can and do become a part of the discipline of education when the educational sociologist is able to organize them into a pattern effective for analyzing and managing group phenomena affecting the operational indices. If this can be accomplished, the basis for reviewing and translating future theory and research of social psychology into a subject matter suitable for use by the educational practitioner becomes a possibility.

As this process develops, the educational sociologist develops greater power to discover how such things as group structure, authority relations, conflict dynamics, group norms, and power relations affect the five operational indices conceptualized as group productivity, group cohesiveness, individual attraction, problem-solving and work contributions, and behavioral integrations or outcomes. In other words, when propositions about the relationships between each of these aspects of group life and the operational indices begin to emerge, these propositions form one kind of content of the discipline of education. As such, these propositions provide a set of principles for analyzing instructional groups when the operational indices are functioning in a manner adverse to the achievement of instructional objectives. In addition, they specify the nature of the changes which have to be made to get the operational indices to function in a manner conducive to the attainment of the instructional objectives.

It must be emphasized that educational practice is controlled or directed by given sets of instructional objectives. These objectives are formulated in keeping with the educational practitioner's judgments about the educational needs or requirements of the society, the importance of certain cultural values, and the educational needs of individuals.[8] Once these educational objectives are established, the educational practitioner then attempts to organize and implement the educational means necessary for learning the behavior stipulated

[7] Gale E. Jensen (ed.), "The Dynamics of Instructional Groups," *National Society for the Study of Education Yearbook* (Chicago: the University of Chicago Press, 1960).

[8] Gale E. Jensen, *The Validation of Aims for American Democratic Education* (Minneapolis, Minn.: Burgess Publishing Co., 1950).

by the instructional objectives. It is at this point, in connection with the analysis, organization, and management of educational means, that sociopsychological phenomena become involved. Specifically, whenever the educational practitioner employs instructional groups as part of his means, sociopsychological knowledge about human groups becomes particularly relevant for the analysis, organization, and management of the sociopsychological group phenomena which are functionally involved in learning the behaviors specified by the instructional objectives. The theoretical propositions and principles which are to be the outcomes of this exposition, therefore, are limited in this example to sociopsychological phenomena related to the operation of instructional groups.

To understand fully the kinds of sociopsychological phenomena which are involved in instructional group situations, we will identify the basic sociopsychological stimuli which produce the kinds of behavior observed in instructional groups. There are two general kinds of such stimuli: one kind is generated by the formal organization which organizes, controls, and supports the instructional group; the other emanates from the personality needs of those who become involved in the roles of instructor and students. Stemming from the dynamics produced by these two kinds of sociopsychological stimuli, which are indigenous to formal instructional situations, there are a number of different kinds of group relationships which inevitably emerge between the members of an instructional group. Theory about these relationships provides the conceptual foundations for educational practice—conceptual foundations which can be utilized to determine how to manage these relationships in ways that will permit the educational practitioner to maintain the operational indices at levels conducive to achieving the educational objectives of the group.

The theoretical definitions of these relationships are borrowed primarily from the field of social psychology. It is this set of definitions that provides the theoretical basis for principles which the practitioner can use to analyze, organize, and control problems of instructional practice. The following paragraphs will provide theoretical definitions for each of the kinds of relationships that can emerge between group members as a result of the dynamics of the sociopsychological stimuli that are generated by the formal organization which organizes, controls, and supports the instructional group, or that emanate from the personality needs of those who become involved as students and instructors.

The first type of relationship that develops between the participants of an instructional group can be identified as problem-solving and work relationships.[9] It is this type of relationship that makes possible the utilization of various instructional procedures and means for developing new perceptual, conceptual, emotional, and motor behaviors specified by the instructional objectives. The instructor chooses his instructional means in keeping with their effectiveness to produce the personal and interpersonal experiences necessary to achieve the new learnings or behaviors. Each time a group member attempts to participate in the planned instructional activities of his groups, he has to rely upon the problem-solving and work relationships that have evolved within the group. It is the effectiveness of these problem-solving and work relationships that determines the progress of an instructional group and the degree to which the instructional objectives will be achieved. Stated otherwise, the established problem-solving and work relationships that have emerged in an instructional group have a direct effect upon the operational indices of group achievement and work contributions. It is because of these connections between the problem-solving and work relationships and the operational indices that the instructor attempts to plan, organize, and control these relationships as means of achieving the perceptual, emotional, conceptual, and motor behaviors specified by his instructional objectives.

A second type of relationship which emerges between participants of an instructional group has to do with decision-making.[10] Instructional groups are constantly confronted with the need for making decisions about such things as the best instructional procedures to use, the kind of learning objectives that should give direction to instructors, the length of time that should be allotted to work assignments, the kinds of policies about examinations that should be followed, the evaluation bases upon which work should be graded, and the kinds and amount of informal friendship activities that should be permitted to develop in the group. Decision-making relationships act as the sociopsychological mechanisms for regulating and con-

---

[9] R. F. Bales and F. L. Strodbeck, "Phases in Problem-Solving," *Journal of Abnormal and Social Psychology,* XLVI (1951), 485–95.

[10] Hare, *op. cit.,* Chap. 3.

trolling the operations of the group. The kind of decision-making relationships that develop seriously affect the effectiveness of the problem-solving and work relationships that are necessary to the acquisition of behaviors specified by the instructional objectives. Moreover, these relationships control the balance between the various types of sociopsychological relationships that develop. It is the decision-making relationship that is intuitively perceived by instructors as extremely crucial to the success of the group. If this kind of relationships fails to function effectively, both the status of the operational indices and the functioning of the problem-solving and work relationships are adversely affected.

A third type of relationship that develops between members of an instructional group pertains to the attempts group members make to influence one another to behave in one way rather than another.[11] Each group member and each instructor has some resources and skills that can be employed to reward or punish others. They use this power, from time to time, to obtain sociopsychological conditions favorable to the attainment of their personal goals. Sometimes they use it wisely, sometimes not so wisely. When used wisely and with the needs of the instructional group in mind, the development of problem-solving and work relationships are facilitated by the personal resources and skills of individual group members. Under these conditions the probabilities for achieving the instructional objectives are greatly increased. However, when personal resources and skills are used unwisely and with no concern for the needs of the group, the problem-solving and work relationships are likely to be less effective. When this happens, the probability of achieving the instructional objectives is lowered. In brief, influence relationships between group members and the instructor can either debilitate or support problem-solving and work relationships. Generally, the instructor has little control over these relationships except as the decision-making relationships act as controls to regulate and influence relationships toward being supportive of the problem-solving and work relationships. For example, if a group member becomes dissatisfied with his experience in an instructional group, he may simply withdraw and thereby withhold resources and skills needed to produce

[11] John R. French and Bertram Raven, "The Bases of Social Power," in Dorwin Cartwright (ed.), *Studies in Social Power* (Ann Arbor, Mich.: The University of Michigan Institute for Social Research, 1959).

the problem-solving and work relationships required for achieving the instructional objectives.

A fourth type of sociopsychological relationship that develops between members of an instructional group evolves from the strong need of members to express to someone their private perceptions and feelings about their personal experience in the instructional group. Whenever the instructional situation intensively affects a member, whether it be through problem-solving, decision-making, influence, or other kinds of relationships that emerge between members, strong inner reactions are produced. This provokes a need to examine and assess personal reactions to the instructional experience. The gratification of this need requires a kind of relationship with other group members which permits an informal, confidential expression and examination of personal reactions to the instructional experience.[12] This type of need is of paramount importance to group members and leads them to initiate informal friendship relationships which at times can supplant the problem-solving relationships. Stated in another way, any of the various types of relationships that become established between members of an instructional group can produce a reaction in the group member such as to create a need to have informal friendship relationships with other members. These relationships can at times become so dominant that they will supplant the problem-solving relationships needed for advancing the group toward the instructional objectives.

A fifth type of relationship that emerges between members of an instructional group centers about their attempts to make personal evaluations of one another.[13] Group members are especially sensitive about maintaining and enhancing their academic success and social worth. They undertake careful assessments of one another before determining whether they are willing to initiate and maintain problem-solving and work, decision-making, and/or informal friendship relationships with other group members. It is the character of these relationships that determines whether group members will receive the kind of satisfaction and rewards which will keep them

---

[12] J. M. Jackson and H. D. Saltzstein, "The Effect of Person-Group Relationship on Conformity Processes," *Journal of Abnormal and Social Psychology,* LVII (1958), 17–24.

[13] Leon Festinger, "Informal Communication in Small Groups," in H. Gutzkow (ed.), *Groups, Leadership and Men* (New York: Carnegie Foundation for the Advancement of Teaching, 1951), pp. 28–43.

involved and encouraged to a degree that keeps them contributing to the group and working to learn the behaviors outlined by the instructional objectives.[14] This type of relationship can easily fractionate an instructional group and create barriers between its members so as to make extremely difficult, if not impossible, the establishment of effective problem-solving and decision-making relationships.

With the completion of the definitions specifying the various kinds of relationships that emerge between members of an instructional group, it now becomes possible to state a set of principles which specify how the different types of group relationship variables must function to assure that the operational indices will be maintained at a level and quality satisfactory to the educational practitioner. These principles have been formulated in keeping with the process outlined in this chapter. They include examples of propositions about the general sociopsychological relationships which need to prevail in instructional groups and examples of propositions pertaining to the management and control of the different kinds of relationships that become established between group members and affect the operational indices employed by the educational practitioner to determine how well the instructional enterprise is proceeding. In brief, these principles represent the culmination of the translation process. As such, they represent knowledge that has been reorganized into forms which can be utilized by the educational practitioner to deal with the problems he encounters in educational situations.

The theory and research studies which were utilized to formulate the principles were obtained from the following sources:

Berelson, Bernard, and Gary A. Steiner, *Human Behavior: An Inventory of Scientific Findings.* New York: Harcourt, Brace & World, Inc., 1963.

Cartwright, Dorwin, and Alvin Zander (eds.), *Group Dynamics and Theory,* New York: Harper & Row, Publishers, 1960.

Hare, Paul A. (ed.), *Handbook of Small Group Research.* New York: The Free Press of Glencoe, Inc., 1962.

Jensen, Gale E. (ed.), "The Dynamics of Instructional Groups," *National Society for the Study of Education Yearbook.* Chicago: The University of Chicago Press, 1960.

Stogdill, Ralph H., *Individual Behavior and Group Achievement.* New York: Oxford University Press, Inc., 1959, Chap. 6.

[14] John W. Thibaut and Harold H. Kelley, *Social Psychology of Groups* (New York: John Wiley & Sons, Inc., 1959), Chap. 12.

Thibaut, John W., and Harold H. Kelley, *Social Psychology of Groups.* New York: John Wiley & Sons, Inc., 1959, Chap. 12.

Principles Pertaining to the General Sociopsychological Conditions Needed for Effective Operation of Instructional Groups.

1. For group productivity (or achievement) and behavioral integration (or learning) to be maintained at a level and quality satisfactory to the educational practitioner, the psychological tension of group members must be maintained at a level which permits the release of energy into problem-solving and work interactions at a rate required by the learning projects and objectives set for the instructional group and its individual members.[15]

2. For group productivity to be maintained at a satisfactory level in adult instructional groups, the various kinds of relationships that develop between group members must be balanced so as to insure that most of the energies of the group members and instructor are channeled into problem-solving and work interactions.[16]

3. For group cohesiveness to be maintained in a manner satisfactory to the educational practitioner, the group norms developed to regulate the behavior of adult learners must facilitate (not inhibit) full participation by group members in the instructional enterprise.[17]

4. For behavioral integrations and group productivity to be maintained at a satisfactory level, learners must assume full responsibility for their participation in the instructional enterprise in a manner that provides the most effective contributions toward successful completion of group instructional projects and the personal achievement of instructional objectives.

5. For group cohesiveness to be maintained at a satisfactory level, disruptive behavior by group members must be perceived by the instructor and other members of an instructional group as a manifestation of a deficient learning situation, until other evidence shows conclusively that such behavior results from some form of deviate personality or behavioral disorganization.

6. For group cohesiveness and individual work and process contributions to be maintained at a satisfactory level, learners, as well

---

15 Cf. Edwin J. Thomas, "Effects of Facilitative Role Interdependence on Group Functioning," *Human Relations,* X (1957), 347–66.

16 Cf. A. Dorwin Cartwright and Frank Harary, "Structural Balance: A Generalization of Heider's Theory," in Cartwright and Zander, *op. cit.,* Chap. 37.

17 Cf. Cartwright and Zander, *op. cit.,* pp. 177–79.

as instructors, must assume responsibility for maintaining the integrity of the instructional group even under conditions of personal frustration, intermember disagreement, and low quality of group performance.[18]

Principles Concerning the Control and Management of Problem-Solving and Work Relationships.

1. For behavioral integrations to be maintained at a satisfactory level and quality, the gratifications or rewards group members experience from participating in the instructional group must result primarily from problem-solving and work relationships leading to the acquisition of new behaviors, rather than from gratifications received from prestige, influence, and friendship relationships.
2. For group productivity to be maintained at a satisfactory level, cooperative (rather than competitive) problem-solving and work relationships must be developed between students.
3. For group cohesiveness and behavioral integrations to be maintained at a satisfactory level, the problem-solving and work relationships between group members must provide for the use of effective "public" methods of evaluating learning progress of individual members.

Principles Concerning the Guidance and Control of Decision-Making Relationships.

1. For group cohesiveness to be maintained at a satisfactory level, the authority and decision-making relationships between group members and instructors must be such that members participating in an instructional group do not experience a loss of self-direction.
2. For individual attraction to remain at a satisfactory level, the level of aspiration for new learnings proposed for a given time period for an instructional group must represent a decision which takes account of the feelings and wishes of the group members.

Principles Concerning the Control and Management of Social Influence Relationships.

1. For individual attraction to be maintained at a satisfactory level, group members must be able to influence the kind of learning

[18] Cf. Thibaut and Kelley, *op. cit.*, pp. 186–87.

projects chosen for the instructional group as a means of making certain that these projects take account of their problems and their needs and abilities to participate.

2. For group cohesiveness to be maintained at a satisfactory level, the instructor must not use his authority in an arbitrary or coercive manner should group members not fully accept his proposed learning projects and instructional procedures.

Principles Concerning the Control and Management of Social Acceptance or Personal Evaluation Relationships.

1. For behavioral integrations to be maintained at a satisfactory level and quality, group members must have full social acceptance by instructor and fellow learners for the release of the energy required for the achievement of the instructional objectives.

2. For individual work and process contributions to be maintained at a satisfactory level, learning projects designed for group members must be commensurate with the participatory and study skills they possess, so as not to confront them with a situation in which a loss of personal esteem is likely to result.

Principles Concerning the Control and Management of Informal Private Interactions.

1. For group cohesiveness to be maintained at a satisfactory level, group members must be free to have informal private relationships with one another whenever the content of these relationships is concerned with attempts to interpret experiences resulting from the problem-solving and work interactions.

2. For group cohesiveness to be maintained at a satisfactory level, members of instructional groups should share the content of informal private interactions with the instructor whenever they feel it secure enough to do so.

The above principles result from employment of the translation process when relevant theory and research is available from other disciplines. As pointed out earlier, these principles place heavy emphasis upon the practical aspects of knowledge in that they give meaning to and order concepts in ways that give better practical control over those variables associated with the learning problems with which the educational practitioner is confronted. Like all, or at least most, of the substance or content of a discipline, these principles will be in some way inadequate, erroneous, or distorted, and therefore will need to be continuously reappraised and corrected. These corrections or reformulations are made possible through systematic study of the consequences of acting on such knowledge in practice situations, and through research and theoretical study projects designed to test and improve them.

In summary, educational sociology becomes a unique discipline or a field of professional study when it is able to translate relevant knowledge of other disciplines into propositions amenable to use by the educational practitioner, and to subject these propositions to testing and revision when practice or research reveal their inadequacies.

Another, but more limited, example describing the borrowing and reformulation of knowledge by the educational sociologist for the educational practitioner can be provided by the area of formal organization as it pertains to educational systems. This will describe certain details not contained in the illustration on instructional groups. One of the perennial problems of concern for educational practitioners has to do with the effect that the size of an educational organization has upon teachers and students. This problem is often manifested through teacher and student satisfaction, absenteeism, and turnover.

A research study from the field of sociology which was concerned with the size of organization and its effect upon individual attitudes and behaviors has developed some theory and research findings that can be used to formulate knowledge which will enable the educational practitioners better to understand and possibly better to manage these problems.[19] In the paragraphs that follow, we will utilize this study as an educational sociologist would—to translate the theory and findings into propositions which are usable by the educational practitioner. The practical problem before the educational practitioner has to do with whether he should attempt to control the size of an educational organization and, if so, what is the optimum size he should attempt to establish.

The stated purpose of the study was to examine (1) how certain organizational processes mediate and affect the influences of size

---

[19] Sergio Talacchi, "Organization Size, Individual Attitudes, and Behavior: An Empirical Study," *Administrative Science Quarterly* (December, 1960), 398–420.

on employee satisfaction and behavior, and (2) the nature and direction of the association between size and employee attitudes.

A theoretical framework for formulating the hypotheses to be tested by the study was outlined as follows:

> Size affects role interaction; role interaction affects attitudes; and attitude affects behavior.
>
> If an organization increases in size, then increases in division of labor and status differentiation will occur which, in turn, will reduce employee satisfaction.
>
> An increase in size will have a differential impact on the satisfaction levels of employees and will vary from one worker to another.
>
> A. Size will decrease an employee's nonmaterial rewards, while increasing his material rewards.
>
> B. In terms of morale, a lowering of satisfaction will increase absenteeism, turnover, and other behavioral correlates of dissatisfaction, viz., restricted output and reduced quality of workmanship. Utilizing this theoretical framework, the researcher formulated the following hypotheses:
>
> 1. In general, employee satisfaction is inversely related to the size of an organization.
> 2. As the size of an organization increases, the amount of satisfaction employees derived from certain organizational experiences is affected as follows:
>   (a) Satisfaction with each of three interpersonal relations experiences (employee-management, employee-supervision, and employee-employee) decreases.
>   (b) Satisfaction with nonmaterial or psychological job rewards decreases more than any of the interpersonal experiences identified under (a).
>   (c) Satisfaction in the area of material rewards does not decrease as organization size increases.
> 3. The level of employee satisfaction is inversely related to turnover and absenteeism.

The research findings of the study were as follows:

1. Hypothesis 1 was significantly supported. More specifically a correlation of −0.67 was found between organization size and the general level of employee satisfaction. Such extraneous variables as the type of economic activity in which the organization engaged or the size of the community in which it was located had no statistically significant effect upon the general level of employee satisfaction.
2. Hypothesis 2(a) was supported.
3. Hypothesis 2(b) was found to be affected by the type of economic activity in which the organization was engaged. The rate of em-

ployee satisfaction with psychological rewards decreases much more rapidly in nonmanufacturing organizations as the size of the organization increases.
4. No significant relation was found between level of satisfaction and turnover.
5. A significant negative relationship was found between level of satisfaction and absenteeism.

With this theory and research evidence, the educational sociologist is now able to make the same kind of approach to the reformulation of this knowledge as was exemplified in the previous example pertaining to instructional groups. When he carries out this task, principles of the following kind become possible:

1. If the size of an organization increases, division of labor and status differentiation tend to increase accordingly and teacher and student satisfaction tends to decrease, to the detriment of organizational productivity.
2. If the size of an organization increases but the role functions attached to jobs are broadened rather than narrowed, teacher and student satisfaction tends to be maintained and productivity heightened.
3. If the size of an organization is accompanied by institutionalization of interdepartmental meetings, internal conflict tends to be averted.
4. If the size of an organization is increased, but the number of hierarchical levels is kept constant via the use of "assistants," internal equilibrium tends to be maintained.
5. If the increase in size of an organization is not accompanied by changes in the structural relationships between roles, teachers and students tend to experience dissatisfaction over both the psychological reward aspects of their work and their interpersonal relations, to the detriment of organizational productivity and security.

These, then, are the kinds of propositions or operating principles that the educational sociologist can supply to the educational practitioner. As these propositions are tested in educational practice, the educational sociologist will be able to determine the kinds of revisions and corrections that are needed to improve them. As new theory and research results become available, the educational sociologist can also revise and improve them. In some instances, when neither new theory and research nor experience resulting from practice is capable of leading to their revision and improvement it will be necessary for the educational sociologist to organize and conduct a program of theory development and research to accomplish this purpose, especially if they are related to an area of educational practice which long has needed improvement.

The Axiomatic Method as a Knowledge Formation Procedure

To establish and maintain a comparative basis for describing the three different procedures for knowledge formation available to the educational sociologist, we will make use of phenomena pertaining to human groups. There are three dimensions of these phenomena to which sociological and social psychological researchers usually address themselves. These can be identified as problems of group structure, problems of group dynamics, and problems of group culture or norms.

In terms of developing knowledge usable by the educational practitioner in instructional situations, investigations of all the different kinds of problems that emerge in each of these general dimensions of group phenomena are not necessarily relevant. Therefore, the educational sociologist needs to limit himself to those aspects of group structure, group dynamics, and group culture that have some kind of bearing upon the organization and conduct of instructional groups. The first step is to identify a subfield of the social psychology of human groups which has high potential for the development of knowledge relevant to educational practice. Because the instructional group constitutes one of the main means employed by the educational practitioner to achieve the behaviors specified by educational objectives, the subfield of investigation is the social psychology of instructional groups. Specifically, this means that the focus of this area of study is upon the matter of human learning as it takes place in these particular kinds of groups. This means that the unit under study or observation will be the instructional group as it may be found in various kinds of organizational and social settings. Data for the exploration of research questions and for the verification or confirmation of hypotheses must come from these kinds of groups. Concepts for theory development must be defined in ways that coordinate with the empirical phenomena to be found within these groups.

To formulate a minimally adequate initial axiomatic theory about the social psychology of instructional groups, it will be necessary to include and investigate variables which provide some representation of each of the three general dimensions of problems to which research workers in the area of the social psychology of human groups address themselves. Eleven variables important to the study of instructional groups—and which represent the dimensions of group structure, group dynamics, and group culture and norms—have been selected to form the basis of an axiomatically formulated theory about human learning in instructional groups.

The next step will be to formulate a frame of reference that will serve as the conceptual basis and starting point for the theory. This framework stems from certain generally accepted meanings about the terms *human group, group structure, group dynamics,* and *group culture and norms.*

The meanings generally attached to these terms are:

1. A *group* is a social unity which consists of a number of individuals who, at a given time, are interdependent in terms of specified relationships and interaction and which, explicitly or implicitly, has a set of standards or norms that regulates the behavior of individual members with respect to matters of importance and consequence to the group.
2. *Group structure* refers to the perceptual and action agreements that exist between group members about the different ways in which they are interconnected with each other.
3. *Group dynamics* refers to the character of the motivations and behavior interactions that take place between group members during their attempts to build and implement a group structure and culture satisfactory to the members.
4. *Group culture* refers to the agreements between group members about what behavior, perceptions, emotions, ideas, and values are proper for members to hold, prefer, and display.

The frame of reference will be composed of the following items:

1. Basic concepts
2. Assumptions
3. Formally defined concepts
4. Operational definitions of concepts or indicators

The basic concepts (primitive or undefined terms) for developing a theory about human learning in instructional groups are as follows:

1. Human individual
2. Group
3. Structural relationship

4. Norms
5. Interaction

The assumptions about instructional groups to be incorporated in the framework represent logical assertions about the basic concepts concerning their nature and interrelationships. These logical assertions are considered to be self-evident:

1. Individuals become members of groups.
2. Groups establish boundaries for themselves. This enables them to determine who is and who is not a member. These boundaries can be determined, and can be either completely closed or permeable in different degrees.
3. Individuals, in becoming members of groups, establish both temporary and persisting relationships between themselves; these constitute the structure of the group.
4. There are a limited number of structural relationships that members can establish among themselves.
5. Different group members establish different patterns of structural relationships between themselves. Individual members will endeavor to establish those relationships that are most rewarding to them.
6. Members are required to initiate and carry on interactions with one another to carry out the work necessary for achieving group goals and fulfilling individual needs.
7. The various kinds of interactions that individual members can conduct with one another are limited.
8. Different members will initiate and endeavor to establish within the group those kinds of interactions that are most rewarding to them. These are not always compatible with the needs of the instructional group as a whole.
9. Individuals, in becoming members of a group, are required to behave according to the norms or behavioral standards which designate the proper kinds of behavior to be maintained by members of the group.
10. Groups may establish behavioral standards or norms that are incompatible.
11. Individual members will try to get the group to establish those standards and norms that are most rewarding to them. These may not always be compatible with the kinds of behavioral standards needed to insure the progress and security of the group.
12. That which is known is observable either directly or indirectly.
13. Some of that which is observable is measurable.
14. That which can be measured can be analyzed through numerical and statistical procedures.

With the identification and statement of these basic concepts and assumptions, the specific variables to be used in the formulation of the theory will now be identified and formally defined. There are eleven of these variables, and they represent concepts derived from the basic concepts and assumptions:

1. *Authority structure.* The degree to which agreement about the allocation of responsibility for decision-making exists in the group.
2. *Problem-solving* and *work structure.* The degree to which group members are willing to assume responsibility for performing the problem-solving functions needed by the group and agree upon work plans and the allocation of work assignments for achieving the instructional objectives.
3. *Achievement of instructional goals.* The degree to which behaviors proposed by the instructional objectives are learned by the members of the group.
4. *Personal prestige structure.* The degree to which individual members are able to maintain a sense of personal worth or prestige position in the group.
5. *Aspirational level.* The degree to which individual members aspire to achieve the behaviors specified by the instructional objectives of the group.
6. *Tension level.* The degree to which members respond to educational means and procedures as psychological stimuli designed to produce the optimal degree of psychological arousal necessary for achieving the instructional objectives of the group.
7. *Reward distribution rate.* The degree to which the rate of reward distribution is satisfactory to group members.
8. *Group-needs norms.* The degree to which the needs of the group take precedence over the needs of individuals during the period when work plans for achieving the instructional objectives are being implemented.
9. *Emotional support.* The degree to which individual members provide emotional support and encouragement for one another to undertake the instructional tasks.
10. *Individual values or needs norms about achievement and work.* The degree to which achievement and work has high importance for group members.
11. *Social influence.* The degree to which group members utilize their personal resources and skills to facilitate (rather than impede) the group work plans designed to achieve the instructional objectives.

It is to be recognized, of course, that in attempts to formulate a theory of instructional groups, variables other than the ones identified and defined above may be utilized. This is a matter of choice, which depends upon the insight and wisdom of the person who is formulating the theory. The central idea of the axiomatic method is to design a theoretical system from which it is possible to deduce or develop hypotheses which contain new or previously unperceived relationships. Specifically, the immediate objective is to develop hypotheses about human learning in instructional groups which enable us to perceive previously unknown facets and relationships about this kind of educational practice. A basic feature of axiomatic theoretical models is that given $(n—1)$ postulates or axioms (when n equals the number of variables of the theoretical system) and granting that all variables appear in at least one of the $(n—1)$ postulates or hypotheses, then all other hypotheses within the system can be determined or derived. The total number of postulates and derived hypotheses, therefore, can be expressed as $\frac{n\ (n—1)}{2}$. Thus, in our proposed axiomatically stated theory about human learning in instrumental groups, which contains eleven variables, there will be fifty-five hypotheses.

The postulates, or basic hypotheses, of this axiomatic model represent assertions about relationships that exist between the eleven variables and have been formulated on the basis of existing research or empirical knowledge. These postulates are stated in such a way that all possible logical relationships between the variables of the system can be deduced from them. An additional requirement is that none of the individual postulates can be deduced from a combination of any two other postulates.

An Inventory of Postulates or Basic Hypotheses

The postulates, or basic hypotheses, of the theory are propositions about the nature of the relationships between the variables as supported by existing research studies. Before selecting a set of propositions that will constitute the postulates of the theory, we must make an inventory of as many propositions as can be readily identified. This inventory will contain propositions of two general kinds. The first consists of groups of propositions in which the same dependent variable is present, but the independent variable is always different. The second is comprised of groups or propositions in which the independent variable is always the same, but the dependent variable is always different. Zetterberg speaks of these inventories as "an inventory of determinants" and "an inventory of results."[20] From these inventories the postulates for an axiomatic theory of human learning in instructional groups can be formulated. Given the eleven variables identified above, this system is capable of providing fifty-five propositions or hypotheses about human learning in instructional groups which can be used as problems to be confirmed or denied by research projects.

Examples of a group of propositions which would be included in an inventory of determinants follow:

1. The higher the status of the authority structure variable, the higher the status the problem-solving and work structure will be. (If *Au* is high, then *PrSl* and *WK* will be high.)
2. The higher the status of the personal prestige variable, the higher the status the problem-solving and work variable will be. (If *PP* is high, the *PrSl* and *WK* will be high.)
3. The higher the status of the aspiration level variable, the higher the status the problem-solving and work variable will be. (If *AL* is high, then *PrSl* and *WK* will be high.)
4. The higher the status of the group-needs norm variable, the higher the status of the problem-solving and work variable will be. (If *Grp Nds N* is high, then *PrSl* and *WK* will be high.)
5. The higher the status of individual needs for achievement and work, the higher the status the problem-solving and work structure will be. (If *Ind Nds Ach* and *WK* is high, then *PrSl* and *WK* will be high.)
6. The higher the status of the social influence variable, the higher the status the problem-solving and work variable will be. (If *SI* is high, then *PrSl* and *WK* will be high.)
7. The higher the status of the emotional support variable, the higher the status the problem-solving and work variable will be. (If *ES* is high, the *PrSl* and *WK* will be high.)
8. The higher the status of the tension level variable, the higher the status the problem-solving and work variable will be. (If *TL* is high, then *PrSl* and *WK* will be high.)

Examples of a group of propositions which would be included in an inventory of results follow:

1. If the status of the authority structure variable is high, the status of the social influence variable will be high. (If *Au* is high, then *SI* will be high.)

[20] Hans L. Zetterberg, *On Theory and Verification in Sociology* (Totowa, N.J.: The Bedminster Press, 1963), Chap. 3.

2. If the status of the authority structure variable is high, the status of the tension level variable will be high. (If *Au* is high, then *TL* will be high.)
3. If the status of the authority structure variable is high, then the status of the achievement of instructional objectives will be high. (If *Au* is high, then *AIO* will be high.)
4. If the status of the authority structure variable is high, then the status of the group needs variable will be high. (If *Au* is high, then *Grp Nds* will be high.)

This, then, is the procedure by which inventories of propositions can be developed. From these inventories certain promising propositions can be drawn to constitute the basic hypotheses or postulates for an axiomatic theory.

From this set of postulates it becomes possible to derive theorems or derive hypotheses about the relationship between the variables. Hans Zetterberg[21] identifies and describes two methods for deriving such propositions: "reduction by definition" and "propositional reduction." Usually the two are done simultaneously. So as not to make this discourse too complicated or burdensome, however, the following attempt to illustrate the development of new theorems or propositions of an axiomatic theory will be confined to propositional reduction.

From propositions incorporated in inventories of determinants and results about human learning in instructional groups, we might identify the following propositions, postulates, or basic hypotheses as those to be used in the remainder of our example:

1. If the aspirational level variable increases, the problem-solving and work variable will increase. If the degree to which the aspirations of group members to achieve the behavior specified by the instructional objectives increases, the degree to which group members (a) are willing to assume responsibility for performing the problem-solving functions needed by the group and (b) agree upon work plans and assignment will also increase.
2. If the problem-solving and work variable increases, the achievement of instructional objectives variable will increase. If the degree of willingness of group members to fulfill the problem-solving and work needs of the group increases, the degree to which group members will achieve the instructional objectives will also increase.
3. If the problem-solving and work variable increases, the achievement and work norm variable will increase. If the degree of willingness

[21] *Ibid.*

of group members to fulfill the problem-solving and work needs of the group increases, the degree to which members will accept the achievement and work norm as a standard of the group will also increase.

4. If the achievement and work norm variable increases, the achievement of instructional objectives will increase. If the degree to which group members accept the achievement and work norm for the group increases, the degree to which members will achieve the instructional objectives will also increase.

From this group of four propositions which one might find in inventories of determinants and results, Postulates 1, 2, and 4 will be chosen to demonstrate the method of propositional reduction as a way for evolving new propositions about the variables that are encompassed by the theory. These, it will be remembered, act as postulates or basic hypotheses for the theory.

If *AL* increases, *PrSl* and *Wk* will increase.
If *PrSl* and *Wk* increases, *HIO* will increase.
If *Ach* and *Wkn* increases, *AIO* will increase.

5. If *PrSl* and *Wk* increases, *Ach* and *WkN* increase. The ability to derive this proposition from two of the postulates is the reason for not including it as a postulate or basic hypothesis. (This, it will be remembered, is one of the requirements for the development of an axiomatic theory.)

Utilizing Postulates 1 and 2, the following theorem or derived hypothesis emerges:

6. If *AL* increases, *AIO* will increase. This is a new proposition and, as such, brings to light a new relationship between the variables of the theory that previously had not been perceived.

Utilizing Postulates 1 and 4, the following theorem emerges.

7. If *AL* increases, *Ach* and *WkN* will increase.

This, also, is a new proposition and provides us with additional insights as to possible relationships between variables.

These new propositions or theorems, of course, will need to be verified or confirmed. Sometimes existing research data can be used as first attempts at confirmation. At other times it will be necessary to launch new research to acquire evidence for confirming or denying the newly derived propositions. Another possible approach to confirmation is through educational practice. The propositions can be checked against the educational practitioner's experience and, if seemingly supported, they can be further checked by having the practitioner direct his action in accordance with them to determine whether the asserted relationship really exists.

At any rate, the axiomatic method has great potential for the educational sociologist in terms of his endeavors to formulate new and improved knowledge for effective and efficient educational practice.

Evolving Principles of Practice from Experience

Perhaps the kinds of propositions that emerge from this knowledge-development procedure, although not particularly elegant in appearance, are the ones that educational practitioners are most inclined to utilize. The educational sociologist can benefit a great deal from a careful examination of this procedure. Most likely, however, he will neglect it, as a potential area of investigation. As a result, the educational practitioner attempts, without benefit of sociopsychological conceptualization, periodically to formalize his experience and to follow his own counsel as to how this formulization should be done and the form it should take. In terms of the standards of the behavioral sciences, these propositions lack an air of respectability and often lead to the erection of barriers between the educational practitioner and the behavioral scientists (and the educational sociologists in particular). The point to be recognized and accepted by the educational sociologist is that these propositions represent to the educational practitioner a kind of knowledge that works. This suggests that he has uncovered some cause-and-effect or functional relationships to which the educational sociologist should become sensitive and perhaps examine intensively for discovering new propositions and testing old ones.

The following paragraphs will be directed to outlining and describing the different phases of this kind of knowledge development. Having accomplished this task, we shall attempt, through illustration, to indicate how it works. This approach generally assumes some kind of goal-oriented operation and the effective and efficient management of a set of means needed to achieve the goals. More specifically, there is always a set of educational objectives to be accomplished and these objectives are achieved by effectively and efficiently utilizing a set of educational means, such as an instructional group. The educational practitioner has to design a series of acts that promise the accomplishment of the educational objectives and he has to maintain a kind of equilibrium within the instructional group that will not jeopardize the attainment of the objectives.

Given this set of circumscribing conditions, the educational practitioner proceeds to carry out his plan of instructional action. Invariably he encounters deficiencies and obstacles in the instructional situation. These deficiencies and obstacles debilitate his action plan and may at times subvert it completely. While keeping an eye on his objectives and action plan, he attempts to remove—or at least to control—these deficiencies and obstacles. Only if he is able to overcome the deficiencies and obstacles encountered at various steps in his action plan, will he be able to move to the subsequent steps. In his history as an educational practitioner, he will encounter these deficiencies and obstacles time and again. If he cannot remove—or at least control—them, he is likely not to achieve his educational objectives (something he finds quite frustrating and upsetting).

Over a period of time, numerous kinds of deficiencies or obstacles appear often. They come to be identified and anticipated by the educational practitioner. In some instances he is able to devise ways to manage them, perhaps profitably, in accomplishing his educational objectives. After he has encountered these situations repeatedly, he is able to generalize about them and perhaps is able to verbalize and record them. These generalizations take the following form:

> Wherever *X* (the deficiencies and obstacles) appears, or is to be prevented, and *Y* (the desired conditions for delivering the educational objectives) is wanted, the introduction of *A* (the corrective or preventive action), will prevent *X* or change it to *Y*.

It is imperative that every educational practitioner formulate these kinds of principles. Without them, it is not possible for an educational practitioner to survive. Mostly, he formulates these kinds of principles unconsciously. As a consequence, they are not likely to be subjected to critical evaluation and subsequent revision, even though at times they work poorly and are seriously in need of revision.

The following paragraphs will endeavor to further clarify this knowledge-development procedure by providing an example. Teachers, through various curriculum-development procedures, work out objectives for various kinds of instructional groups. This, then, makes the instructional group a goal-oriented instructional mechanism. It is implicitly recognized by the teacher that the instructional group provides the basic means for the achievement of the instructional objectives. It is the way in which the teacher conducts and manages the instructional group that will determine the degree to which the instructional objectives will be achieved. Given a set of instructional objectives (behaviors to be acquired by the group members or students), the teacher devises a plan of operation or action based on his psychological and subject-matter knowledge about what conditions have to be instituted in order to facilitate the learning of the behaviors specified by the objectives. As he attempts to implement this plan, to employ the most effective instructional procedures and techniques available to him, he encounters deficiencies and obstacles in the instructional group which prevent the group from making progress toward the achievement of the educational objectives. Specifically, four kinds of obstacles and deficiencies encountered in instructional groups are: (1) fear to try to learn, (2) apathy or lack of incentive to learn, (3) loss of personal prestige when attempts to learn are publicly unsuccessful and cause a subsequent withdrawal, and (4) inability to prevent disagreement from turning into conflict. These are four kinds of obstacles and deficiencies that every educational practitioner has encountered, for they appear very frequently in the learning situation. Almost every educational practitioner, through trial-and-error methods, has tried to correct them. Occasionally, a practitioner is successful in preventing or correcting some of these situations. After experiencing such success, he is pleased with his efforts and attempts to determine just what was done to prevent or correct the situation. In a loose, informal way, he formulates for himself a series of "if . . . then" kinds of statements which he attempts to follow when he senses they are applicable. These "if . . . then" statements constitute the practitioner's teaching secrets. Very often he intuitively formulates them in such a way as to take full advantage of his personality and teaching skills and obtain the most effective implementation of his principles in the instructional situation. Typical examples of these instructional principles would be as follows:

1. If it is important for students to be willing to try to learn new and sometimes difficult behaviors, and if the instructor wishes to avoid

instructional situations in which students are fearful and, therefore, unwilling to try to learn new behaviors, the instructor must by verbal policy and instructional action create an atmosphere in which students encourage and support one another to undertake new learning ventures.

2. If it is important for students to want to become and remain involved in class learning projects, and if the loss of "face" or respectability prevents a student from doing so, it is important for the teacher to make certain that members of a class learn to refrain from depreciating fellow class members.
3. If it is important for members of an instructional group to utilize their disagreement about ideas, issues, values, and action as a means of utilizing the uniqueness of individual members to further learning, and if disagreements which lead into conflicts tend to divert the attention and emotions of group members from the learning project into angry attacks upon one another and enduring dislike for one another, then the teacher should make certain that the degree to which members like and respect one another is strong enough to keep disagreements centered around the learning projects of the group.

Thus we see that these kinds of propositions and principles of practice stipulate, first, the conditions desired and needed within the group to achieve the instructional objectives (goals of the group); second, the conditions to be prevented or corrected; and third, the action that must be taken to avoid or correct the situation. Very often the preventive and corrective actions are synonomous. It simply depends upon whether the group has more of *X* or *Y* at the beginning of its existence and how it "slides" toward *X* or *Y* during its existence.

This knowledge-development procedure, unlike the other two, is largely under the control of the practitioner. In its simplest form it can be described as a procedure of evolving propositions or principles about educational practice based upon the practitioner's trial-and-error experiences while (1) trying to institute the conditions he wants, (2) trying to prevent or eliminate the conditions he does not want, and (3) specifying what has to be done to accomplish this. It is most unfortunate that these propositions exist only in the minds of educational practitioners. If they were recorded, they would provide rich material for the educational sociologist. Certainly this suggests that the educational sociologist should give some attention to these kinds of endeavors in the future.

Summary

This chapter was concerned with identifying and describing three knowledge-development procedures that are applicable to the field of educational sociology. The first procedure was the reformulation of sociological knowledge in a way that makes it usable by the educational practitioner. The steps for accomplishing this task were outlined and examples provided which showed how knowledge of small groups and formal organizations could be reformulated so as to enable the educational practitioner to diagnose the problematic group and formal organization situations with which he is confronted and to devise and implement plans of action that would be effective for accomplishing his learning objectives in situations in which group and formal organization factors are influential. The second procedure was the axiomatic method. The significance of this procedure for educational sociology was discussed and an example was provided as to the way in which it could be used to develop knowledge that the educational practitioner could use in practice situations in which small or face-to-face group phenomena were involved. The third procedure consisted of evolving principles of practice from experience. The discussion entailed an account of how knowledge is developed through this procedure and also an example of how the procedure could be used to develop knowledge the educational practitioner could use to cope with problems with which he is continuously faced in the instructional group.

All these knowledge-development procedures can and should be used by the educational sociologist. Each has its strengths and weaknesses, its advantages and disadvantages. At times the use of one of the procedures will promise greater and more rapid progress in the development of educational sociology knowledge needed by educational practitioners; at other times, one of the other procedures may hold greater promise. The important thing in the long run, however, is that knowledge developed by one procedure can be checked against that developed by either or both of the other procedures.

CHAPTER IV

Research Planning for Developing Educational Sociology as a Discipline

Generally speaking, little thought ever has been given to determining the nature of the educational research that is needed to develop the kinds of knowledge needed for improving educational practice. It is true, of course, that a goodly amount of effort has been given to identifying research areas and problems within these areas that need to be investigated to advance the field of professional education. Little time and energy, however, has been given to the requirements that the research enterprise itself should meet if the knowledge is to be useful to or usable by the practitioner. Historically, there has been a naïve notion that all that has to be done is to conduct research and then all problems will be solved. This notion has been prevalent in the thought of educational researchers and practitioners for many years, contributing to the frustration and disappointment that has been experienced about the results of educational research.

The main objective of this chapter, therefore, is to analyze and make proposals about the kind of requirements that any research undertaken by educational sociologists should meet if it is to be concerned not only with worthwhile substantive problems, but also with employing research designs that make it possible to formulate the kinds of practice principles needed by the educational practitioner. Briefly, educational sociology should avoid studies which, because of the way they investigate the problem, can not provide usable knowledge for the educational practitioner. This does not preclude pure or basic research studies. It only asserts that research on educational problems should aim at the development of propositions which are usable in dealing with problems of educational practice. The research to be planned and conducted by the educational sociologist clearly should be governed by this criterion.

To meet the main objectives of this chapter, three kinds of discussions are needed. First, there is a need for developing a rationale which, for research planning, manifests the main theses of the book and provides a descriptive account of the sequence of steps that would be involved in planning and conducting research. Second, there must be an analysis of research problems which identifies the different general types or levels of problems and the kind of research findings that can be expected from each. Third, there is need for a discussion of the kinds of research designs that can be appropriately used with the different general types or levels of research problems. Very little thought has been given to this aspect of educational research. This lack probably accounts for the surprise and disappointment that result from research for which there was high hopes, but which produced rather obvious, mundane findings.

A Rationale for Research Planning for Educational Sociology

For the educational sociologist to plan and conduct research in a manner consistent with the way this book has described and prescribed the work of this field, it will be necessary for him to be consciously aware of and familiar with a research planning rationale and procedure that is grounded in the main ideas of the book.

The first step is to determine or identify perennial problems of educational practice (see Chapter II). This requires the educational sociologist to keep his clinical ear tuned to the situations in which the educational practitioner is endeavoring to take effective educational action. More specifically, the educational sociologist should develop an inventory of these perennial problems and then continually sift through them for purposes of reorganizing and restating them in more effective ways and relating them to both old and new research studies and theories of a sociopsychological nature. This will keep the educational sociologist constantly in touch with and grounded in the field of educational practice. It also will force him to review the theoretical and research literature and to make inquiries of theorists and researchers trying to order sociopsychological phenomena conceptually. It is this activity that enables him to determine which of the various knowledge-formation procedures described in Chapter III might be most appropriate for developing new propositions needed by the educational practitioner. In some instances, he may become aware of theory and research that enables him to utilize the borrowing-and-reformulation procedure. In other instances, he may be able to identify and state in an effective way a series of propositions that have evolved from the experience of practitioners. At other times he may decide that entirely new theory and research problems will have to be formulated. The important thing is that whatever procedure he chooses, so long as he takes cognizance of this step, he will start at the right place and he will have firmly established and consciously understood the base from which to make his choices about the basic nature of the research and knowledge-development procedures that would be most appropriate and economical.

The second step is to assess the various kinds of perennial problems with the objective of determining both the general and specific areas of problems that would be most crucial for obtaining improvement in educational practice. There doubtless are numerous general problem areas and specific problems within each of these areas which, if explored properly and the results utilized skillfully, would contribute in an important way to the advancement of educational practice. There is, however, little doubt that some general problem areas and the specific problems contained therein have greater potential than others for making revolutionary advances. The function of this step, then, is to order the perennial problems into those categories or areas which seem to contain similar problems. When this has been accomplished, each of the general problem areas and the specific problems contained therein can be analyzed in terms of their respective potential for producing changes which could improve educational practice. There is always, of course, the possibility that a mistake could be made in judging the potential of each area for advancing educational practice, but this seems to represent no greater hazard than choosing problem areas and specific problems within each by chance and personal-preference procedures. At least the procedure being proposed provides some way of assessing progress in terms of alternatives and, therefore, a chance to shift emphases to another problem area should an area that had been judged to be of high potential not fulfill the expectancies of the researchers. When the different problem areas or categories have been identified and some analysis and assessment of their potential to advance educational practice has been made, they can be ranked in some order of priority which portrays the results of the assessment.

The third step should be concerned with speculations about the kind and theoretical quality of propositions that will be needed as conceptual foundations for reconstructing educational practice. Heretofore, we have not concerned ourselves with what kinds of findings and propositions are necessary for reconstructing educational practice in ways needed to improve practice. Usually, we merely develop some findings, formulate whatever propositions we can from them, and then assume that any educational practice that would be based upon them would represent an improvement. In brief, it is assumed that whatever emerges from research is better than what we now have and, in fact, represents the way in which the phenomena involved actually behave. When one reviews changes in child-rearing and educational practices that have evolved from the child-development studies of the last forty years, along with the discrediting and rejection of traditional practices built on hundreds of years of human experience, one wonders whether these changes really represent an improvement or a setback. The point to be made is that it is necessary to give some thought to the kinds and quality of findings and propositions that are needed if educational practice is to be enhanced. This does not come about automatically. To be specific, if the principle or proposition needed to improve some area of educational practice requires statements that portray cause-and-effect relationships between the variables or factors involved, then the formulation of statements which merely provide a picture of the status of these variables at a given time are of little use.

There are three general kinds of questions an educational practitioner faces:

1. What is the educational situation in which I am working like, and what are the educational consequences it is producing?
2. What, if anything, can and should be done to correct or improve the situation?
3. How should the action for correction or improving the situation be accomplished?

Each of these kinds of questions requires different kinds of research findings and propositions. In order to obtain change, sometimes it is one kind of question that needs the greatest emphasis, sometimes another. Whichever it is, the findings and propositions resulting from research must be of the kind that fit the type of question most strategic for advancing educational practice. To produce findings and propositions which are relevant to one of the other kinds of questions is simply to produce frustration and disillusionment.

Once the educational sociologist has some notion of the kind and theoretical quality of the findings and propositions needed to reconstruct educational practice, he is in a position to identify the kinds of research problems that would be strategic for producing those findings and propositions. It is this task that constitutes the fourth step in research planning for the educational sociologist. In recent efforts to allocate financial support for different kinds of research proposals, one question usually posed is: How significant is the research for the field of education? This question is usually directed to the substantive aspects of the research problem as formulated or stated in the research proposal. Little attention is given to the character of the formulation of the research problem itself as an aspect of the significance of the research. The different general types of questions with which the educational practitioner is confronted require that research problems be formulated in different ways if the kinds of findings and propositions needed to reconstruct educational practice are actually to materialize. In many instances research problems are formulated in the wrong way in terms of the general question that is most strategic for the reconstruction of practice.

The fifth step is to determine the kinds of study approaches or strategies, research designs, and data-analysis procedures and techniques that would be required to explore the chosen research problems in a way that will produce the kind of findings and propositions identified as necessary for reconstructing strategic areas of educational practice. The production of the right kind of findings and propositions can be realized only if the right problems and the right kinds of research approaches, designs, and procedures are properly coordinated. If the wrong kind of instruments and/or data-collection procedures are used, even though the research problem is the right one, the research findings required to reconstruct or improve educational practice will not be possible. If the wrong kind of sampling designs and procedures and/or the wrong kind of handling of the independent or experimental variables is utilized, the kind of propositions specified for improving educational practice becomes impossible. Thus, the choices made at this step represent the operationalization of the previous decisions and must represent the logical projections or prior steps, or the findings and propositions needed for improving educational practice cannot be achieved.

The sixth step is to survey the present level of knowledge development in the different problem areas identified and described in Step 2. The task here is to discover the discrepancy that exists between the level of findings and propositions needed to improve or reconstruct educational practice and the present or existing level of findings and propositions (assuming that some have been developed). This task requires the educational sociologist to examine the character of the theory being used in the different problem areas; to review the research results and findings; and to assess the research strategies, designs, sampling procedures, data-collection procedures, and data-analysis plans that were utilized to explore problems in the different areas. It is from this kind of work that the educational sociologist is able to make some kind of judgment as to how great the discrepancy is between what now exists in the way of knowledge development and what is needed if the improvement or reconstruction of educational practice is to become a reality. If the existing development of knowledge in a given area contains generalizations or propositions, these too have to be assessed in terms of their logical and empirical validity. Sometimes these propositions have been accepted as being true simply because they were stated at the end of a research report. Unfortunately, they are sometimes learned and accepted by the educational practitioner and he may attempt to base his practice upon them even though they are extremely inadequate and sometimes downright unworthy as knowledge upon which to base educational practice. Perhaps we have instituted more bad educational practice in this way than in any other way devised thus far. It is now time that the educational sociologists recognize this and take steps to correct it.

The seventh step has to do with determining how much time and how much investment would be needed to raise the present level of the problem area to the level, both in terms of verification and propositions, required to bring about the desired improvement in educational practice. In other words, the task at this step is to determine what sort of investment is needed to eliminate the discrepancy between the present level of development in a given problem area and the proposed or needed level of development required for improving educational practice in that area.

The eighth step the educational sociologist should follow in planning his research has to do with determining which problems should have the highest priority. This entails a review of the different problem areas that have been identified and analyzed in the first seven steps and then ordering them into some kind of priority which specifies the ones that should be given attention first and to what degree. The kinds of analyses that are provided by the preceding steps can provide both data and criteria for making judgments as to the order of priority the different problem areas should be given. From previous work it is clear that some areas will have greater potentiality for bringing about significant changes in educational practice that would represent improvement over what we now have. Previous analyses will also show how large the discrepancy is between what we now have and what we should have, and what degree of effort would be required to close the gap. Sometimes it may be necessary to settle for lesser goals and actually achieve them rather than to try to achieve something that would require an impossible effort in terms of resources, skills, and technology. Some kinds of research may require far too long a period of time, and we may decide to try to obtain lesser improvements in practice because they can be achieved in a shorter period of time. Knowledge development in some problem areas may be at a high level and to raise it to the desired level may be a small task requiring less investment in time, energy and money. Some problem areas will have better developed theory and research technology and greater experience with translating theory and research into practice. This fact may lead to a decision to put a great deal of effort into this problem area, or it may lead to the opposite, depending upon whether some other area happens to be judged as more significant for obtaining improvement in educational practice. The significant point is that the educational sociologist at this point has to review the results of his previous steps and then judge the problem areas most strategic for educational practice and the society, and the levels to which knowledge development in the different problem areas should be raised in order to improve educational practice so as to make a satisfactory contribution to the community and society. He must also judge how much of a discrepancy exists between the present level of knowledge development and the needed level for each problem area; how much of an investment of time, energy, and financial support is needed to close the gap or discrepancy between the present knowledge level and the needed level; and whether it is reasonably possible in light of existing theory and research technology to close the gap. He must determine how much time would be involved and decide whether such an amount of time can be afforded. He must survey available human, material, and financial resources and then make a judgment as to whether the amount and kinds of resources would be adequate for successfully eliminating the discrepancy that exists between present and needed knowledge for improving a given problem area. Finally, he must decide which problem areas should get what amounts and kinds of resources for what periods of time. From this series of judgments a priority listing of problem areas and research problems will emerge. Furthermore, this priority list should be commensurate with the kinds and amounts of resources available to carry out these research projects.

The ninth and last step, then, becomes one of determining the best research strategy to employ to implement the research projects for which resources can be gathered. In brief, the final question is that of determining how best to employ available (and usually scarce) resources to obtain not only the greatest amount, but also the most strategic, improvement in educational practice. In some problem areas it may be better to devote time to theory development; in others, to inventing new research methods, techniques, and measuring scales. In some areas, problems of data analysis may be the stumbling block and therefore may require whatever resources can be allocated to the study of such problems. In other problem areas it may be best to take existing research theory and findings and invest available resources into endeavors directed toward developing new forms of educational practice. This would be followed by research designed to test whether the newly designed forms of practice will work in the way expected and to discover how they might be revamped to work more effectively.

From the sequential procedure outlined above, the following rationale for planning educational sociological research emerges. First, the problem areas for educational sociology research should result from observations of what happens when one set of human beings trys in some systematic way to maneuver another set of human beings into learning given or designated behaviors. It really does not make too much difference whether this phenomenon takes place in school or not. The significant phenomena involved are organizational forms, instructional acts, and teaching technology that are introduced and utilized by one group of persons to induce in another set of persons a set of behaviors that are desired by at least one of the groups. The educational sociologist should focus particularly upon what might be termed the sociopsychological aspects of this organizational, instructional activity and technology with the objectives of describing in an accurate, meaningful way to the educational practitioner what is taking place; identifying a number of alternative lines of actions the practitioner might take in dealing with the situation and which of these possibly represents the best organizational, instructional, and technological policies in terms of the values and aspirations of the society; and identifying how the different alternatives might be accomplished, along with an evaluation of their effectiveness and efficiency. The responsibility of the educational sociologist, however, should not end here; rather, he should attempt to identify the new kinds of practice and the new kinds of knowledge that are needed to make such practice work. That is, he must set forth new forms of educational practice to be developed and specify the level of knowledge that is to be achieved as a means of realizing them. It may be that the educational practitioner will not always agree with these objectives, but this is just what is needed in order to maintain continuing analyses about the directions that efforts to improve educational practice should take. Very often educational practitioners will be inclined to adopt a very practical and short-sighted view of their problems. In other cases the educational sociologist may take to "sailing in the clouds" and propose new forms of practice that, because of their unattainability at the time, simply force the educational practitioner to continue what he is doing at present. The history of practical and technological change is full of both kinds of examples. It is the responsibility of the educational sociologist to make certain that we learn something from history and that we do not squander our resources on either too low or too high a level of aspiration.

Once the sights for new and improved educational practice have been set, the educational sociologist should begin the development of a plan which incorporates the research strategy, tactics, and logistics necessary to move toward the new objectives set for educational practice. Presumably the educational sociologist is not quite as much encumbered by problems for immediate action as the educational practitioner is, and he should devote some time to thinking years in advance of where educational practice and its foundational knowledge is. This means that he should be prepared to propose not only the various and best ways to fight the battle, but the most effective and least costly as well. Logistically, he must have a plan that makes certain that when something is needed, it is at the right spot at the right time. Many fine research projects have turned out to be dismal failures, not because they were ill conceived or because the research tactics being employed were inadequate or poorly chosen, but rather because the logistical plan which was used to support the research strategy and tactics was faulty.

This, then, is the rationale behind the procedures previously outlined for the educational sociologist as he pursues his task of planning research. It is planning which is concerned with the systematic investigation of sociopsychological phenomena, but it also is planning which focuses upon sociopsychological phenomena as these can be observed when one set of humans attempts to utilize human organization, instructional interactions, and instructional technology to get another set of human beings to learn a given set of behaviors desired by either or both.

General Types of Research Problems in Educational Sociology

The popular notion among educational practitioners is that "a research problem is a research problem." It is true, of course, that it is important to ask the right questions and to develop them in a skillful way. Little thought, if any, however, has been given to the fact that there are levels of research problems that determine the kinds of findings that will emerge, and the kinds of propositions that can be formulated from the research.[1] If particular kinds of propositions are needed to improve a given form of educational practice, but if the research problem is not formulated at the level which permits the formulation of these kinds of propositions, then the re-

---

[1] Hans L. Zetterberg, *On Theory and Verification in Sociology* (Totowa, N.J.: The Bedminster Press, 1963), Chap. 1.

search cannot produce the kinds of propositions needed to improve the given form or area of educational practice. A goodly share of past educational research seems to have been directed by a level of problem formulation that cannot produce either findings or propositions necessary for the kinds of conceptual foundations for changes in educational practice. So long as researchers continue to formulate the kinds of educational problems that have been so prevalent during the past twenty and thirty years, there is little hope that educational research can make any difference for educational practice.

This is a problem that has confronted the educational researcher for at least twenty years. The educational researcher has been acutely aware that his work has contributed little to educational practice. In rather feeble ways he has tried to overcome it by writing practical pamphlet-type publications for educational practitioners which outline what educational research indicates about educational practice. In brief, he has attempted to tell what his research suggests with respect to the way educational practice might be conducted. Very often this turns out to be a laboring of the obvious. For twenty years or more he, also, has persuaded thousands of educational practitioners to take "consumer" educational research courses, the objectives of which were not to teach the practitioner how to conduct educational research but, rather, how to read educational reports and continuously utilize educational research findings to improve his practice. This placed the burden of translating research findings and improving educational practice wholly upon the educational practitioner.

Neither of these activities for utilizing research to improve educational practice seems to have worked very well, and for the most part educational practitioners have proceeded to formulate their own ideas and principles about how educational practice should be conducted. In doing this they have relied primarily upon the third kind of knowledge formation procedure outlined in Chapter III. Occasionally, some especially insightful, sensitive, and knowledgeable practitioner or textbook writer would perceive something in a research report and be able to utilize it for improving educational practice. It is safe to say, however, that the improvement of practice through the utilization of educational research was essentially a matter of chance.

The point to be made at this juncture is that the time has come for the educational sociologist, through his research planning, to overcome this deficiency. There is little likelihood that the educational practitioner, with his constant concern for taking action, ever will be in a position to perceive this deficiency accurately or to do anything about it. As it is, the practitioner over the years has done by far the most sensible thing with respect to knowledge formation: he has developed principles of practice based on those things that he knows are in some way functionally related and that make a difference to his client. If the educational researcher is ever to be able to say as much for himself, the chances of improving educational practice would be greatly increased.

If one examines a wide variety of research problems and then reflects on their nature, he will perceive that if problems are formulated in different ways—even though they be investigating the same things—the results simply are going to report different findings about the same things. This is certainly not a wondrous statement; it is simply something that any researcher, even the least sophisticated novice, knows. The point is that we have never bothered to determine the implications of this known fact for developing or formulating propositions upon which educational practice rests. The reason is probably that we started from problems of practice and were never really interested in determining what sociological research might offer in the way of new propositions that would make a difference in educational practice.

Research problems about the educational sociological aspects of educational practice can be stated at five levels. The level chosen depends upon the results that emerge from the previously described rationale and the procedures for planning educational sociological research.

There are problem areas in which very little is known about the nature of the sociopsychological phenomena involved. It may be relatively certain that phenomena of a given kind are involved, but it is difficult to identify them, much less describe them in any perceptive way. But this particular area is a strategic one for improving educational practice. This means that it must be investigated. It also means that one must start from scratch. There are no concepts, no data-collection instruments or measurement scales, no designs or ways to analyze data that might emerge from a study organized to explore such phenomena. Whenever this is the case, the research problem is one which has to be formulated to uncover something about the nature of the phenomena; at least one hopes to learn enough to develop a nomenclature that will make it possible to identify and name the parts. The development of a nomenclature is the basic requirement for a researcher and a practitioner in any intelligent discussion about the phenomena and ultimate speculations about them and their behavior under certain conditions when in the presence of other kinds of phenomena. This is the first level of research problem formulation. The level at which a problem is formulated has nothing whatsoever to do with the respectability or whether it is a "high" or "low" science. Research problems have to be formulated at all the levels that will be identified; it is the wise researcher who knows at what level his problem should be formulated to obtain the kinds of findings that are needed. Often the "respectability needs" of the researcher have led to the development of senseless research problems in terms of developing findings and propositions needed by the educational practitioner. The educational practitioner often has intuitively recognized this and politely proceeded with the job of "running the shop" in a way that he knows will work.

The second level of research problem is concerned with determining the status of or the amounts in which certain factors exist in given situations and under given conditions. To formulate a research problem of this kind means that there exists a nomenclature and the various factors can be identified so as to organize a study which attempts to establish how much or how many of the various factors or parts exist. This is the sort of thing survey studies attempt to do. It is an important kind of research problem for the educational practitioner because it often provides him with an outline of the elements and their organizational relationships in the situations in which he has to work. These kinds of problems also provide him with some notion of the proportions in which the various elements exist. Although, perhaps, these kinds of findings cannot be used to formulate propositions which indicate how different factors affect one another or the propositions an educational practitioner must ultimately possess if he is to take action with some insight, they nevertheless can provide propositions which portray the base or starting point from which the practitioner must organize his efforts. These kinds of propositions are much more important to the educational practitioner than most educational sociologists realize. Usually the educational sociologist is inclined to strive for the kinds of research findings that will permit him to formulate propositions which organize variables into some kind of functional relationship to one another. There is no doubt that he should and must strive for these latter kinds of propositions, because without them the educational practitioner can never hope to improve or change practice situations except by intuitive approaches. These latter kinds of propositions, however, are developed rather slowly and the practitioner cannot wait until they are available. Furthermore, the propositions that emerge from the findings of these second-level problems often suggest the hypotheses from which confirmed theoretical propositions are later developed.

The third level of research problem is concerned with discovering which factors might possibly have some kind of link with one another. Like the second-level problems, a definite nomenclature of factors connected with the phenomena is or needs to be available. The main task of these third-level problems is that of determining which of these factors seem to change and/or begin to exhibit certain kinds of behaviors when others are changing or exhibiting specified behaviors. There is no assumption or underlying evidence in these types of problems that the factors have any cause-and-effect relationships to one another. Problems of this kind lead to the organization of studies which sort the various identified factors of a given kind of phenomena to determine the character of variation taking place in the different factors at some given point in time. In a sense, the researcher is looking for possible trends or concomitant variations among the factors. If the researcher is able to discover any such concomitant variations, he will try—through various types of data analysis—to uncover the statistical nature of the associations. When he is able to establish with a high degree of statistical frequency an association between certain factors, he begins to think that there is possibly some kind of cause-and-effect or functional relationship between two or more factors. However, this kind of research problem primarily yields statistical evidence of relationships between the factors under study.[2]

The findings from this third level of research problem can be

[2] This is beautifully illustrated in the present scientific arguments as to whether smoking is the "cause" of the high rate of lung cancer.

utilized to formulate hypothetical propositions that have great significance for educational practice. Although they are not as yet empirically confirmed, these hypothetical propositions can be checked against the clinical experience of the practitioner. Very often they will provide the practitioner with a "missing link" which enables him to explain why certain unexpected consequences to his actions appeared. Improvement in educational practice does not always have to wait for fully empirical confirmed propositions because practice rests at least as much (or more) upon slowly accumulated, intuitive generalizations or unconsciously held propositions from experience as it does upon propositions derived from research. Whenever a practitioner is able to gain new insights about the relationships between factors involved in educational practice, he is able to conduct his practice in a more skillful manner. Thus, hypothetical propositions based primarily upon statistical evidence can be helpful to him. These kinds of propositions are, of course, especially helpful to the educational sociologist in his research planning, for he can use them as the bases for formulating some kind of integrated theoretical system and for organizing research studies designed to discover empirically whether certain factors do have a cause-and-effect relationship upon one another.

The fourth level of research problem has as its objective the empirical confirmation of some kind of cause-and-effect or functional relationship between two or more of the factors of the phenomena being studied. Usually this means that the research study will be organized in some experimental form. It is at this level of research that the problem of control becomes paramount. On the basis of statistical evidence there may be very strong support for asserting that two or more of the factors are linked together. The fourth level of research problem is one which has to demonstrate that this is so and that the behavior of the factors is in fact a consequence of the linkage between them and not the result of some unexpected but known, or unknown factors. It is the part that unexpected known and unknown factors can play that creates the problem of control. The findings of these kinds of problems should enable the educational sociologist to make judgments as to whether there are or are not linkages between the factors being studied in the research problem. If there is some thought on his part that the behavior of one of the factors under study could have been produced by another known outside factor, he indeed would be very reluctant to suggest to the educational practitioner that whenever he acts in a way to affect given factors, he can expect that an *X* factor will respond in some way to this action. These are the kinds of propositions in which the educational practitioner is most interested. It is at the point, when there is little doubt that linkages exist between certain factors, that the possibilities for improvement of educational practice are increased. Even though the nature of the full effects of one factor (or factors) upon another is not known, propositions of this kind enable the practitioner to become an intelligent, systematic observer. He can feel more or less certain that, whenever he takes action designed to affect one or more of certain factors, others will respond. If his action is effective with respect to the factors in which he is interested, he can expect that the other factor or factors will respond in some way and that his next job is to observe whether the factor or factors being affected are acting in a way detrimental or favorable to his instructional or educational objectives. If his instructional actions should prove to be detrimental, he then can attempt to make adjustments in these actions and, mostly by trial and error, to relate the factors to one another in a way that proves to be favorable to the achievement of his instructional objectives. In brief, the findings from research studies of this level make possible the development of the theoretical foundations of a scientific practice.

The fifth level of research problem has as its objective the determination of the nature of the cause-and-effect or functional relationships that are known to exist between the various factors being studied. The fourth-level problem is concerned primarily with establishing whether in fact there exists a functional relationship between the factors under study. As a result, it is not always possible to determine from the findings of these kinds of studies what the nature of the relationships are. For example, is the relationship between Factor *X* and Factor *Y* linear—and, if it is, what is the slope of the line? If the relationship is something other than linear, is the relationship, nevertheless, monotonic? How much of an increment is produced in *Y* when *X* is increased by a given increment? This is a level which educational research seldom, if ever, has reached. Nevertheless, the educational sociologist must aspire to this level because it is attainable. When propositions based on these kinds of findings can be formulated, the educational practitioner should be able to perceive clearly what the significant factors in the instructional situation are and how they will need to be functionally related if certain educational results are to be achieved. He may not always be able to develop an educational practice or program that can take full advantage of this knowledge. This is nothing unusual, however: engineering practices built on the confirmed propositions of the physical sciences are seldom able to use but a very small number of them in terms of developing a beneficial practice. For the good of mankind and from an examination of the present state of the art of warfare, this is probably just as well.

Now that five levels of research problems have been identified of which the educational sociologist should become aware, it becomes possible to reflect briefly on the advancement of educational practice as it tried to utilize educational research as a means of improving practice. The great hope of the educator in the 1920's, expressed many times in the educational literature, was that research would lead the way toward a new and improved practice. The forty years since then have not seen this hope fulfilled. Many experts feel that very little progress has been made toward fulfilling it. As one reviews research recommendations contained in such publications as the *Encyclopedia of Educational Research* and various journals reporting educational research, it becomes fairly obvious that the level of the research problems represented in these publications indicates that the hopes educators had for educational research in terms of improving educational practices were unrealistic.

Designs Appropriate to Different Levels of Research Problems

The research designs to be used with different levels of research problems in educational sociology prescribe and outline the way the research work needs to be conducted to investigate given research problems properly. A research design, regardless of the level of research problem involved, manifests five kinds of highly significant decisions concerning the way in which the research action should and will be conducted. The plausibility of the research findings will be determined by the "goodness" of these decisions.

First, research designs must prescribe in terms of time and place the points at which data collection (or measurements) need to be made with respect to the different variables incorporated in the research problem. Some studies will collect data on certain variables more than once; others will not. Some will collect data on the variables simultaneously; others will not. Some will collect data on all variables of the problem; others will not. The point is that different types of research problems will require that data be collected on different variables, at different times, in different places, in different sequences, and from different subjects. The research design must provide an effective and efficient rationale and data-collection schedule in accordance with the research problem to be investigated.

Second, research designs must provide for the phenomena incorporated in the study to operate in a way that permits the research problem to be studied properly. The central question has to do with whether the phenomena under study need to operate in some specified, theoretically contrived, manipulated way or whether they should operate in a natural, spontaneous manner. That is, some problems to be investigated properly require the phenomena involved in the study to operate according to some theoretical specifications that may or may not require manipulation of designated variables of the problem; other problems need the phenomena under examination to operate in a spontaneous, unmanipulated way. The former type of problem is often an experimental one for which the research design must identify and implement experimental treatments for a given variable or variables of the study. An important feature of research designs for problems which will involve experimental treatment of given variables is that of prescribing the points at which experimental treatment of the given variables is to be introduced and the period of time for which it is to run.

Third, research designs must provide for the handling of extraneous variables; i.e., those variables that could account for the findings of the study just as well as the independent variables contained in the formulation of the research problem. This is often identified as the control problem. In some kinds of research studies, the development of this feature of research designs is a simple matter because control of extraneous variables is neither required nor desired. Rather, the problem at hand can best be investigated by letting the factors involved interact with whatever other factors are present in whatever way they spontaneously may do so. Other kinds of research studies require vigorous control of extraneous variables and a specification of the conditions that are to prevail during the period in which data on the status and behavior of the variables are being collected. The methods by which this control is accomplished seem to be of three general kinds. First, there is control by the physical exclusion of extraneous factors. That is, the research design is of such a nature that the undesired extraneous variables are physically and psychologically excluded from the study. Laboratory studies by physical scientists, the use of "germ-free" animals by biological scientists, and experimental studies by physiological psychologists provide examples of this method. A second method is control by specification. When this method is employed, the extraneous variables are not excluded; rather, their status and function (e.g., whether they are to remain constant or whether they can interact and vary according to specified patterns) during the study are specified. In other words, the specific way the known extraneous variables are to operate during the study are identified. It is assumed that whatever is discovered about the research problem will hold whenever extraneous variables operate in the specified way. The study of the effects of different kinds and quantities of fertilizers under different conditions of sunlight, moisture, and temperature provide examples of this method of control. Another example is provided by experimental instructional studies which specify the status of academic achievement and I.Q. variables of the subjects to be used in the study. The third method of control might be called one of statistical estimation. This method employs experimental-statistical designs which provide for the randomization of both subjects and experimental treatments of given variables as a means of statistically estimating the probability that known and unknown extraneous variables and/or chance alone might have produced the research results rather than the independent variables of the research problem.

Fourth, research designs for educational sociology need to provide for continuity of observation and data collection to whatever degree required to study the research problem properly. Some research problems require an extensive amount of time with data being collected continuously at more diffuse points over a long period of time; others may require the collection of data at some single point from a cross-section of the phenomena involved. Designs which provide for the former kinds of observation and data collection will be designated *long-run longitudinal designs;* the latter, *short-run cross-sectional designs.* The former kinds of designs enable the researcher to keep the variables under study for an extended period of time to collect data about their quantitative status and behavior as the phenomena being examined evolve from one stage or phase to the next. Sampling surveys exemplify short-run cross-sectional designs. These would be at the low end of a continuity scale. Human-development studies tend to exemplify long-run longitudinal designs. They would be at the high end of a continuity scale. Research problems in educational sociology that arise from the different types of perennial problems of the educational practitioner are likely to require the use of both short-run cross-sectional and long-run longitudinal designs. Although it is quite likely that the findings from longitudinal designs will be more plausible or acceptable, there will be many instances in which short-run cross-sectional designs will be not only necessary but also quite acceptable for investigating the research problem properly.

Fifth, the research design needs to provide for findings that can be utilized to formulate generalizations or propositions about the nature and behavior of the variables of a research problem that will be valid at places and times other than those at which the study was conducted. The underlying question connected with this feature of research design is: How representative are the research findings about the nature, status, and/or behavior of the variables of a given research problem in terms of what would be discovered about them in other times and places under similar conditions? How certain can we be that what was discovered about these variables at the time and place the study was conducted would be the same as might be discovered at other times and places whenever similar conditions are present? Many of the older disciplines handled the problem of representativeness simply by replicating research studies; i.e., by having different researchers study the same thing in the same way and by doing studies on the same problem. Sometimes research workers, unaware that another worker was studying the same or a similar problem, would arrive at the same or similar kinds of research findings. This certainly helped to increase the representativeness of the findings. The development of sampling theory and techniques has provided another approach to this problem. It has been used widely by the behavioral sciences in dealing with the problem of representativeness and it is now common to find in reports on research studies a section which identifies the sampling problem of the study and describes the sampling procedures and techniques employed to deal with it. There is no doubt that when a research design systematically provides for a sampling plan for dealing with the problem of representativeness of the research findings, the plausibility of generalizations or propositions based on these findings is increased. Although there is no doubt that the replication of studies is still highly desirable and that the field of educational sociology should provide for this approach to the problem of representativeness, serious attention given to sampling during the development of research designs can save a great deal of time and increase the plausibility of the representativeness of the findings.

Having identified the central items involved in the development of research designs in general, it is now possible to determine the requirements the designs for different levels of research problems, as they are found in educational sociology, would have to meet. The following discussion of this matter does not make any distinction between so-called descriptive-inductive and hypothetico-deductive approaches to research. The underlying notion of this presentation is that whether a researcher perceives himself as employing one or the other approach, his decisions about designs will need to meet the requirements that have been established for the different levels of educational sociological research problems. The designs might be different if a researcher decides to use one approach rather than the other but, regardless of which approach he decides to employ, the designs he develops to investigate his problem should meet the prescribed requirements for designs for the different kinds of research problems.

First-level research designs must make it possible to determine effectively and efficiently under natural, spontaneous, unmanipulated conditions what the substantive elements and components of given unknown phenomena involved in a research problem are and what they do or how they behave (i.e., what their behavioral properties are). Consequently, the specification of the times and places at which data need to be collected is done in keeping with the intuition, hunches and impressions of the researcher, particularly if there are to be opportunities for data collection. The main question with respect to this feature of these designs is whether there are to be predetermined times and places for data collection or whether the researcher is given the prerogative of collecting data at times and places he feels or judges would be most revealing. Because the conceptual or theoretical formulation of this level of research problem is often unrefined and unsystematic, it is difficult to determine just when and where one is likely to obtain data that will reveal something about the nature of the phenomena involved. When the study is to run over a fairly long period of time and a great deal of opportunity for data collection is available, it might be possible to set up regularized time intervals in which to collect data. The researcher can simply ride along with the situation and observe and collect data at will. However, when this is not the case, it is necessary to rely upon the intuition and judgment of the researcher as to where and when the most informative data could be collected. Simply stated, the research is trying to map the phenomena involved and the criterion as to when and where data should be collected is that data should be collected whenever and wherever it becomes possible to do the most accurate mapping job.

With respect to the way the phenomena should operate to study a problem properly, designs for this level of research problem should provide for the phenomena to operate in a spontaneous, unmanipulated way. If the researcher is to develop realistic perceptions and ideas about the nature of the phenomena, his research must not interfere with the natural unfolding of events. At this level of research the researcher has little understanding of the phenomena to which he is devoting his investigatory efforts. His task is patiently to wait for them to reveal something about their nature (something about their elements, organization, and behavior) and then to observe skillfully and record accurately what happened. Any tampering with the natural unfolding of events is likely to create an inaccurate picture or record or at least one which is very difficult to interpret. If the phenomena are to be mapped accurately, they must operate in their typical, spontaneous, unmanipulated (by man) way. Premature manipulation of unknown phenomena can lead to the distortion of results and consequently to inaccurate perceptions and misunderstanding about the nature and behavior of the phenomena.

Research designs for this level of research problem need not make any provision for the control of extraneous variables. The problem of controlling extraneous variables really does not exist for this kind of research problem. One cannot realistically classify variables as independent, dependent, and extraneous. The research is primarily concerned with an accurate identification and description of the elements, structures, component systems, and behavioral properties of the substances and events that appear. The basic questions directing inquiry are: How can the phenomena be described? What are their elements and properties? What developmental and behavioral features or characteristics appear when and where? In a sense, nothing is extraneous; there is nothing to be eliminated, controlled, or estimated as to its influence.

Pertaining to continuity of observation and data collection, research designs for this level of problem should provide, whenever possible, for long-run longitudinal rather than short-run cross-sectional study. In many instances the phenomena being studied will manifest some kind of developmental and/or behavioral cycle. When this is the case, the research design should provide for continuity to the extent that it will operate long enough to cover one or more cycles, depending on the length of time it takes to complete a cycle. The main thing is to provide the researcher with an opportunity to observe the phenomena pass through the different phases or stages of their developmental or behavioral cycle. At times, however, the researcher may wish to study one phase or aspect of the developmental or behavioral cycle rather intensely. In this case the use of short-run cross-sectional designs is quite appropriate. Also, whenever a developmental cycle covers a long period of time, it may be both necessary and convenient for the researcher to conduct a number of short-run cross-sectional studies of different phases of the cycle.

The problem of providing for representativeness is not particularly difficult for, and really is not relevant to, the development of research designs for this level of problem. Because longitudinal long-run designs will be one of the dominant features of most designs developed for this level of research problem, the problem of representativeness is handled almost automatically in that replication is likely to be implicit or inherent in most longitudinal designs in which there is more than one case and more than one developmental or behavioral cycle. The employment of sampling to this level of research problem as a means of dealing with the problem of representativeness is not particularly meaningful and may possibly lead one astray by obtaining a sample of things that are not part of the unknown phenomena under study. In other words, it may lead the researcher to study the wrong things.

The second level of research problem is concerned with determining the quantitative status of certain variables or factors contained in the formulation of the research problem. Second-level research designs must make it possible to determine effectively and efficiently under natural, spontaneous, unmanipulated conditions what the quantitative status of defined variables is for a given place and period. In brief, the central purpose of these studies is to determine the quantitative status of given factors or variables for some specific time and place (or, in some instances, a series of times and places). Very often it becomes a matter of determining the quantitative status of some variable or factor just before and/or after some event has taken place; e.g., how much inclination there is in a given population to vote favorably on the passing of a school bond issue two months before the election.

The specification of points and places for collecting data by research designs for this level of problem is one of the most important features. These designs need to provide in detail for the times and places at which data are to be collected on the different variables. It is this feature that places the data into some kind of meaningful setting.

These designs need to make provision for phenomena to behave in a spontaneous, unmanipulated way. As the researcher is primarily concerned with determining how much of something exists, he must establish a relatively passive relationship with the phenomena and try to make a systematic quantitative assessment of the problem variables or factors under natural conditions.

Research designs for second-level research problems do not need to make any provision for the control of extraneous variables. Second-level problems really are not amenable to being formulated in terms of independent, dependent, or extraneous variables. The basic question is: How much of given factors exist at given places and times? Nothing needs to or should be controlled.

To a great extent second-level research designs will be cross-sectional and short-run in character. Because the basic objective behind these kinds of problems is that of portraying and establishing the quantitative status of specified factors at given times and places, cross-sectional, short-run designs are appropriate. Mostly, there is no attempt to uncover anything new about their substantive nature or their functional relationships to each other. Whenever this emphasis changes in second-level problems—that is, whenever something besides ascertaining the quantitative status of the factors incorporated in the problem formulation becomes important—then longitudinal long-run designs need to be provided. These usually take the form of planning for more than one or a series or sequence of measures in the same places. When second-level research designs incorporate longitudinal long-run data-collection and observation features, the chances of discovering something about the substantive nature and behavior of the problem variables is improved.

Providing for the representativeness feature of second-level research designs is a matter of paramount importance. This type of design usually tries to obtain and utilize data from a sample as a means of determining the quantitative status of the problem variables for a much larger group known as the research population. As the objective of these studies is to formulate a series of statements about the quantitative status of the problem variables for a given population, some assurance about the representativeness of the sample is imperative. Research findings about the sample is of little interest unless there is some basis for accepting that they are representative of the research population.

Third-level research designs must make it possible to determine effectively and efficiently under spontaneous, unregulated conditions whether the concomitant variations of given variables of a research problem portray some kind of statistical association.

Points and places at which data should be collected about the variables of the problem must be specifically designated. Generally speaking, data should be collected at those points and places where it is expected, theoretically or intuitively, that the variables are operating in such a way as to show possible statistical relationships. The plausibility of the findings will depend a great deal upon the kind of provision these designs make for data-collection times and places. Implicit in most research designs of this kind is the idea that data on all variables are to be collected under a common set of conditions at approximately the same time. Typically, arrangements are made to collect data on the problem variables from a sample of cases or subjects and then to use the data obtained from the sample cases to determine to what extent the same association pattern would appear in the larger number of cases to which the research pattern pertains. Unless the design makes the proximity of time and place for the different variables clear and reasonable, it is difficult to determine the plausibility of the research findings. If a reasonable degree of proximity of time and place is not evident, the plausibility of the findings is likely to be very low. Specifically, if the proximity of place is not met, there is no way of knowing whether all the variables of the problem were operating in the same social unit under the same conditions. If the proximity of time is not met, there is no way of knowing whether the variables were acting concurrently.

With respect to the way the phenomena should operate to study the variables properly, these designs need to provide for spontaneous, unmanipulated operation. This research is primarily concerned with the discovery of possible relationships between variables. The discovery of statistical associations between variables is the first step. Because the researcher is trying to get some clues as to what concomitant relationships might exist, he needs to permit the phenomena to operate in a spontaneous, natural way. His task is essentially that of collecting data on how specified variables behave in terms of the way they vary concurrently with one another in some given sociopsychological unit or system. The relationships between variables are identified through analysis. There is no attempt to show that variables are causally connected or linked to one another.

Research designs for these kinds of problems do not need to provide for the control of extraneous variables. The problem of controlling extraneous variables does not exist in any experimental sense because studies designed to investigate this level of problem are not aimed at establishing any causal connections or empirical linkages between the variables and the problem. It is merely concerned with discovering what variables seem to "go together."

The provision for continuity of observation and data collection should be for short-run cross-sectional studies. The main objective of these studies is to determine between which variables there is a strong probability or likelihood that some kind of linkage might exist. Once these statistical associations are established, the bases for problems and studies designed to determine whether some kind of empirical causal linkage actually exists can be established. There is no need to continue with these kinds of studies beyond the point where strong statistical associations are evidenced. To continue with them beyond this point may be to perform a disservice to educational sociology unless the nature of the problem is such that experimental studies and/or axiomatic model studies are not possible. Should this be the case, provision must be made for long-run longitudinal designs which develop numerous statistical associations that ultimately might be used as the raw material for formulating axiomatic models which permit the formulation of problems and the conducting of studies concerned with establishing empirical causal linkage between the factors or variables of the problem.

Research designs for this level of problem should provide for reasonable representativeness through sampling whenever possible. It is important that they be as effective as possible in discovering statistical associations. This means that the provision for points and places for data collection is probably the most important feature of these designs and that, if need be, more emphasis should be placed upon it than upon provision for representativeness.

Fourth-level research designs must make it possible to determine effectively and efficiently under specified, sometimes theoretically contrived, and sometimes manipulated conditions whether variables known to be statistically associated are causally linked or connected in a reciprocal or in a unilateral way. Research designs for this level of problem, therefore, are likely to be experimental in character. In those situations in which experimental studies are not possible, but where there is a need to determine whether causal linkages exist, designs which can test the theorems and hypotheses of axiomatic models can be employed.

Whether experimental or axiomatic model designs (or a combination of both) are employed, it is important for the design to provide specifically for the points and places at which data collection on the different variables is to be done. Seldom has enough attention been given to this feature of research designs that have been used to investigate this level of problems. For example, little, if anything, is ever said in research reports utilizing pre- and post-test measures about when the post measure should be made. Usually it is assumed that it should be made immediately after the experimental manipulation of an independent variable or variables. In the event there were a lag between the time the experimental variable is introduced or manipulated and the time the dependent variable reacted fully, data collection on the dependent variable immediately following the experimental treatment might well be premature. This implies that the researcher needs to be clearly aware of what his theory or rationale directing the research suggests as to the proper points and places for data collection. Consequently, designs for this level of research problem need to specify explicitly the points and places at which data collection needs to be made to explore the research problem properly. The plausibility of the findings of the research rest heavily upon this feature of the design.

When experimental designs are used, the phenomena involved in the study will need to operate in contrived, manipulated, and, whenever possible, theoretically specified ways. When axiomatic model designs are employed, the phenomena should operate either in the way they do under experimental designs or, if this is not possible, in a spontaneous, unmanipulated way so long as they operate in accordance with the conditions theoretically specified as being necessary to study the problem properly. The plausibility of the findings of fourth-level research problems depends a good deal upon whether the phenomena being studied operate in the way stipulated as being necessary to create the conditions necessary for proper investigation of the research problem.

Research designs for this level of research problem must carefully provide for control of extraneous variables. As the objective of these studies is to show that two or more variables are causally linked or connected, the plausibility of the findings of the study heavily depend upon whether the observed behavior of the variables of the problem might be attributed to the influence of variables other than those incorporated in the research problem. The techniques to be used to control these outside variables depend, of course, upon what is possible. Control by exclusion is the strongest of the available techniques, but probably will be possible to use least often with educational sociology research problems. Control by specification and/or the holding constant of known extraneous variables can be used effectively whenever known extraneous variables are suspected as having some influence on the behavior of the variables incorporated in the research problem. Control by statistical estimation can be used profitably whenever the sampling procedures used can meet the criterion of randomness and there is concern about the possible influence of unknown as well as known extraneous variables.

Research designs for this level of research problem should be primarily short-run and cross-sectional in character because the main objective of these studies is simply that of producing evidence as to whether given variables are or are not in some way causally linked or connected. All that is necessary in terms of providing for continuity of observation and data collection is to create, or to allow to evolve, the phenomenological conditions specified for studying the problem properly; to introduce and implement (or let naturally evolve) the experimental treatment; and to collect data on the dependent variables(s) at the designated or appropriate times and places. In brief, all that is needed with respect to providing continuity for observation and data collection is to provide for an adequate amount of time properly to conduct the experimental treatment and collect data on the dependent variables(s). As soon as this process has been completed, the study terminates. Some studies, of course, may take longer, but this does not alter the fact that they are short-run cross-sectional studies.

Providing for representatives by these designs, especially by random sampling, should be advanced as far as possible, but only to the point that sampling procedures will not interfere with having the phenomena operate in ways specified for studying the problem properly and with the proper implementation of the experimental treatment. Whenever provisions for increasing representativeness interfere with these two things, they should be eliminated. In other words, whenever provisions for representativeness hinder the phenomena, and especially the experimental treatment, from operating in ways specified as necessary for determining whether the variables of the research problem are causally connected, then attempts to increase representativeness should be terminated.

Fifth-level research designs must make it possible to determine effectively and efficiently under specified, theoretically contrived, and sometimes manipulated conditions the nature of the functional (mathematical) relationships that exist between variables known to be causally connected or linked. Specifically, one of the important things is to discover whether the relationships are linear or curvilinear and, if possible, what the equation is that best describes this relationship. Like the fourth-level research designs, these designs need to be experimental in character and/or need to employ axiomatic models and procedures whenever possible.

These designs must specifically designate the points and places at which data collection on the different variables is to take place. This must be done according to the causal linkage or connections that are known to exist between the variables. It is the accurate plotting of data trends that reveals the nature of the functional relationships between variables. In brief, it is the skill with which points and places can be designated that determines the chances that the functional relationships can be uncovered. If this is not done with a good deal of skill, there is little likelihood that the equations derived from the data will fit the actual relationship that exists between the variables under study. This skill really depends upon the "goodness" of the theory that has been developed by the previous research conducted at the first four levels.

The fifth-level designs need to provide for experimental treatments to operate in specified or contrived ways. When this cannot be the case, a well-known cycle describing how the phenomena behave needs to be specified and then theoretical formulations utilized to predict what is to evolve. At any rate, the important thing is that the phenomena should as much as possible be made to behave in accordance with the conditions required to investigate this kind of problem properly.

Determining the nature of the functional relationships that prevail between the variables of a research problem requires that extraneous variables be controlled as much as possible. Designs for this level of problem should not only control the known extraneous variables, but also enable the researcher to detect the presence and influence of unknown factors. The strongest methods of control possible should be used although it must be recognized that educational sociological problems being researched at this level will seldom be able to use control by physical exclusion. Control by statistical estimation, based on randomizing the subjects of the study and the experimental treatment, probably will have to be utilized a great deal of the time. In those cases where extraneous variables are known to exist, but where neither control by physical exclusion nor control by statistical estimation is possible, control by specification of the status of the known extraneous variables during the study might be employed. This might be the case when an experimental manipulation approach to the study is not possible.

The provision for continuity of observation and data collection of these designs can be short-run and cross-sectional in character. The main requirement for continuity is that they run long enough to collect data which will portray the characteristics of the functional relationships that operate between the variables of the study. In that the phenomena operate in a specified, contrived, or manipulated way, the study needs to be a cross-sectional one, rather than longitudinal. As soon as the conditions specified for the study have run their course and the data collected, the study is completed. This is true whether the study is an experimental one or one structured by the use of the axiomatic method and then employed in a situation in which experimental manipulation is not possible.

As with fourth-level research designs, the representativeness of fifth-level designs should be developed as highly as possible. However, when random sampling procedures constitute the main bases for establishing representativeness, it is important that providing for representativeness does not interfere with the ways the phenomena are required to operate to study the problem properly or with the proper implementation of the experimental treatment. Ultimately the representativeness of findings of fifth-level studies is established through replication rather than sampling.

Summary

This chapter provides the conceptual foundations for the research ventures that may be undertaken to develop the field of educational sociology. Particularly it attempts to establish the requirements that any and all research in educational sociology should meet if the research is to be productive in the sense of being able to develop knowledge that is usable by the educational practitioner. To make these requirements clear, three kinds of tasks were accepted for the section. The first was to develop a research rationale and planning procedure which would manifest the main theses of the book and which should be used for selecting research problems and for guiding research planning for educational sociology. The nine steps of a procedure were identified and discussed. The second task was to identify the different general types or levels of research problems that are found in educational sociology. Five of these were identified along with the kinds of research findings that could be expected to be obtained from each type or level of problem. The third task was to indicate the kinds of research designs that are appropriate for each type or level of research problem. The main features of research designs for educational sociology were described and an attempt was made to specify the kinds of research designs that are appropriate to use with the different levels of research problems.

It might be said that the success of the educational sociologist with respect to developing educational sociology as a distinct and productive field will depend ultimately upon the wisdom and skill with which he is able to employ the thoughts of this chapter. He must possess an adequate rationale and procedure for selecting his research problems and projecting his research planning. To rely only on intuition and chance for carrying out these tasks is likely to be time-consuming and wasteful. The educational sociologist must be aware of the kind of findings the different kinds of research problems can logically produce. A lack of this kind of awareness can lead only to unwarranted hope and disillusionment on the part of the educational practitioner. He must be aware of the kinds of research designs that can be used properly with different kinds of research problems. A lack of this kind of awareness easily can lead to his deluding himself about what he thinks he has discovered.

Bibliography

Amital, Etzioni, *Complex Organizations: A Sociological Reader*. New York: Holt, Rinehart & Winston, Inc., 1961.

Angell, R. C., "Science, Sociology and Education," *Journal of Educational Sociology*, I (1928), 406–13.

Bandura, A., and R. Walters, *Social Learning and Personality Development*. New York: Holt, Rinehart & Winston, Inc., 1963.

Barker, Roger G., and Herbert F. Wright, *Midwest and Its Children*. Evanston, Ill.: Row, Peterson & Co., 1954.

Berelson, Bernard, and Gary A. Steiner, *Human Behavior: An Inventory of Scientific Findings*. New York: Harcourt, Brace & World, Inc., 1964.

Blalock, Hurbert M., Jr., *Causal Inferences in Nonexperimental Research*. Chapel Hill: University of North Carolina Press, 1961.

Blau, Peter M., *Exchange and Power in Social Life*. New York: John Wiley & Sons, Inc., 1964.

Braithwaite, R. B., *Scientific Explanation: A Study of the Function of Theory, Probability and Law in Science*. Cambridge: At The University Press, 1955.

Brown, Robert, *Explanation in Social Science*. Chicago: Aldine Publishing Co., 1963.

Brookover, Wilbur B., "The Relation of Social Factors to Teaching Ability," *Journal of Experimental Education*, 13 (1945), pp. 191–205.

———, *A Sociology of Education*. New York: American Book Company, 1955.

Campbell, Donald T., and Julian C. Stanley, "Experimental and Quasi-Experimental Designs for Research on Teaching," in Gage, N. L., ed., *Handbook of Research on Teaching*. Chicago: Rand McNally & Co., 1963.

Caplow, Theodore, *Principles of Organization*. New York: Harcourt, Brace & World, Inc., 1961.

Caplow, Theodore, and Reece McGee, *The Academic Marketplace*. New York: Basic Books, Inc., Publishers, 1958.

Cartwright, D., and Alvin Zander, *Group Dynamics*. Evanston, Ill.: Row, Peterson & Co., 1960.

Charters, W. W., Jr., "The Social Background of Teaching," in Gage, N. L., ed., *Handbook of Research on Teaching*. Chicago: Rand McNally & Co., 1963.

Dahlke, H. Otto, *Values in Culture and Classroom: A Study in the Sociology of the School*. New York: Harper & Row, Publishers, 1958.

Davis, Allison, *Social-Class Influences Upon Learning*. Cambridge: Harvard University Press, 1948.

Durkheim, Emile, *Education and Sociology*. New York: Free Press of Glencoe, Inc., 1956.

Francis, Roy G., *The Rhetoric of Science*. Minneapolis: University of Minnesota Press, 1961.

Gage, N. L., "Paradigms for Research on Teaching," in Gage, N. L., ed., *Handbook of Research on Teaching*. Chicago: Rand McNally & Co., 1963.

Gagné, Robert M., *The Conditions of Learning*. New York: Holt, Rinehart & Winston, Inc., 1965.

———, "Military Training and Principles of Learning," *American Psychologist,* 17 February (1962), 83–91.

Gordon, C. Wayne, *The Social System of the High School: A Study in the Sociology of Adolescence*. New York: Free Press of Glencoe, Inc., 1957.

Gronlund, Norman E., "Relationship Between the Sociometric Status of Pupils and Teachers' Preferences For or Against Having Them in Class," *Sociometry,* 16 (1953), 142–150.

Gross, Neal, "Problems and Prospects in the Sociology of Education," in *Sociology Today*. Problems and Prospects. Major papers delivered at the 52nd Annual Meeting of the American Sociological Society, 1957. Edited by Robert K. Merton, Leonard Broom, and Leonard S. Cottress, Jr. New York: Basic Books, Inc., Publishers, 1959.

Gross, Neal C., Ward S. Mason, and Alexander W. McEachern, *Explorations in Role Analysis: Studies of the School Superintendency Role*. New York: John Wiley & Sons, Inc., 1958.

Halsey, A. H., and Jean Floyd, *Education, Economy, and Society*. New York: Free Press of Glencoe, Inc., 1962.

Hare, A. Paul, *Handbook of Small Group Research*. New York: Free Press of Glencoe, Inc., 1962.

Havighurst, Robert J., Paul H. Bowman, Gordon P. Liddle, Charles V. Matthews, and James V. Pierce, *Growing Up in River City*. New York: John Wiley & Sons, Inc., 1962.

Herrington, George S., "The Status of Educational Sociology Today," *Journal of Educational Sociology,* 21 (1947), 129–139.

Henry, Jules, *Culture Against Man*. New York: Random House, 1963.

Hines, Vynce A., and Robert L. Curran, "The School and Community Forces," *Review of Educational Research,* 25 (1955), 48–60.

Hollingshead, August B., *Elmtown's Youth*. New York: John Wiley & Sons, Inc., 1949.

Hunter, Floyd, *Community Power Structure: A Study of Decision Makers*. Chapel Hill: University of North Carolina Press, 1953.

Hyman, Herbert H., "The Value Systems of Different Classes: A Social Psychological Contribution to the Analyses of Stratification," in *Class, Status, and Power: A Reader in Social Stratification,* Reinhard Bendix and Seymour M. Lipset, eds. New York: Free Press of Glencoe, Inc., 1953, pp. 426–442.

Janowitz, ed., *Community Political Systems*. New York: Free Press of Glencoe, Inc., 1961.

Jenkins, David H., and Ronald Lippitt, *Interpersonal Perceptions of Teachers, Students, and Parents*. Washington, D.C.: National Education Association, Division of Adult Education Service, 1951.

Jensen, Gale E., "Bureaucracy, Unionization, and Obsolescence in American Educational Organizations," *School of Education Bulletin,* The University of Michigan, 35, No. 1 (May 1963), 1–7.

Jensen, Gale E., ed., *The Dynamics of Instructional Groups.* National Society for the Study of Education. Fifty-Ninth Yearbook. Part II. Chicago: University of Chicago Press, 1960.

———, *The Validation of Aims for American Democratic Education.* Minneapolis: Burgess Publishing Co., 1950.

———, ed., *Socio-Psychological Analysis of Educational Problems.* Ann Arbor: Ann Arbor Publishers, 1957.

———, ed., *Supplementary Readings for Educational Society.* Ann Arbor: Ann Arbor Publishers, 1959.

Jensen, Gale E., A. A. Liveright, and Wilbur Hallenbeck, eds., *Adult Education: Outlines of an Emerging Field of University Study.* Adult Education Association of the U. S. A., 1964.

Jensen, Gale E., and Max R. Goodson, *Formal Organization in School Systems.* Ann Arbor: Ann Arbor Publishers, 1956.

Kerlinger, Fred N., *Foundations of Behavioral Research.* New York: Holt, Rinehart & Winston, Inc., 1965.

Kreitlow, Burton W., "School-Community Relations," *Review of Educational Research,* 25 (1955), 299–318.

Kuhn, Alfred, *The Study of Society: A Unified Approach.* Homewood, Ill.: The Dorsey Press, Inc., 1963.

Lawrence, Paul, and J. Seiler, *Organizational Behavior and Administration* (rev. ed.). Homewood, Ill.: Richard D. Irwin, Inc., 1965.

Lerner, Daniel, ed., *Evidence and Inference.* New York: Free Press of Glencoe, Inc., 1958.

Lerner, David, and Harold Lasswell, eds., *The Policy Sciences: Recent Developments in Scope and Method.* Stanford: Stanford University Press, 1951.

Lieberman, Myron, *Education as a Profession.* Englewood Cliffs, N.J.: Prentice-Hall, Inc., 1956.

March, James, ed., *Handbook of Organizations.* Chicago: Rand McNally & Co., 1964.

McClelland, David C., and others, *Talent and Society.* New York: D. Van Nostrand Co., Inc., 1958.

McEwen, William P., *The Problem of Social Scientific Knowledge.* Totowa, N.J.: The Bedminster Press, 1963.

Merton, Robert K., Leonard Broom, and Leonard S. Cottwell, Jr., *Sociology Today: Problems and Prospects.* New York. Basic Books, Inc., Publishers, 1959.

Moore, Wilbert E., *Man, Time and Society.* New York: John Wiley & Sons., Inc., 1963.

Nagel, Ernest, *The Structure of Science: Problems in the Logic of Scientific Explanation.* New York: Harcourt, Brace & World, Inc., 1961.

Presthus, Robert, *Men At The Top.* New York: Oxford University Press, 1964.

———, *The Organizational Society.* New York: Alfred A. Knopf, Inc., 1962.

Popper, Karl. R., *The Logic of Scientific Discovery.* New York: Basic Books, Inc., Publishers, 1959.

Queen, Stuart A., William N. Chambers, and Charles M. Winston, *The American Social System*. Boston: Houghton Mifflin Company, 1956.

Richey, Herman G., ed., *Behavioral Science and Educational Administration*. National Society for the Study of Education, Sixty-Third Yearbook, Part II. Chicago: University of Chicago Press, 1964.

Richey, Robert W., William H. Fox, and Charles E. Fauset, "Prestige Ranks of Teaching," *Occupations,* 30 (1951), 33–35.

Rosen, Bernard C., "The Achievement Syndrome: A Psycho-Cultural Dimension of Social Stratification," *American Sociological Review,* 21 (1956), 203–211.

Sears, Robert R., Eleanor E. Maccoby, and Harry Levin, *Patterns of Child Rearing*. Evanston: Row, Peterson and Co., 1957.

Sherif, M., C. Sherif, and R. E. Nebergall, *Attitude and Attitude Change: The Social Judgment-Involvement Approach*. Philadelphia: W. B. Saunders, Co., 1965.

Sidman, Murray, *Tactics of Scientific Research*. New York: Basic Books, Inc., Publishers, 1960.

Smelser, Neil J., and William T. Smelser, *Personality and Social Systems*. New York: John Wiley & Sons, Inc., 1963.

Smith, B. O., "New Approaches to Pedagogical Science," *Educational Theory,* I. No. 2 (August 1951), 79–86.

Smucker, Orden, "The Campus Clique as an Agency of Socialization," *Journal of Educational Sociology,* 21 (1947) 163–168.

Sorokin, Pitirim A., *Society, Culture, and Personality: Their Structure and Dynamics*. New York: Harper & Row, Publishers, 1947.

Spindler, George D., ed., *Education and Anthropology*. Stanford: Stanford University Press, 1955.

Staats, Arthur W., and Carolyn K. Staats, *Complex Human Behavior*. New York: Holt, Rinehart & Winston, Inc., 1963.

Stiles, Lindley J., ed., *The Teacher's Role in American Society*. New York: Harper & Row, Publishers, 1957.

Stogdill, Ralph M., *Individual Behavior and Group Achievement*. New York: Oxford University Press, 1959.

Travers, Robert N. W., *Essentials of Learning*. New York: The Macmillan Company, 1963.

Waller, Willard, *The Sociology of Teaching*. New York: John Wiley & Sons, Inc., 1932.

Zaleznik, A., and D. Moment, *The Dynamics of Inter-Personal Behavior*. New York: John Wiley & Sons, Inc., 1964.

Zetterberg, Hans L., *Social Theory and Social Practice*. New York: The Bedminster Press, 1962.

Znaniecki, Florian, "The Scientific Function of Sociology of Education," *Educational Theory,* 1, No. 2 (August 1951), 69–78.

Index